TALKING TRUTH,
CONFRONTING POWER

Discourse Power Resistance Volume 6

Talking Truth, Confronting Power

Edited by
Jerome Satterthwaite, Michael Watts
and Heather Piper

Trentham Books
Stoke on Trent, UK and Sterling, USA

Trentham Books Limited

Westview House   22883 Quicksilver Drive
734 London Road   Sterling
Oakhill   VA 20166-2012
Stoke on Trent   USA
Staffordshire
England ST4 5NP

First published 2008

British Library Cataloguing-in-Publication Data
A catalogue record for this book is available from the British Library

ISBN: 978 1 85856 432 6

Cover: Siobhan Bromley

Designed and typeset by Trentham Print Design Ltd., Chester and printed in Great Britain by Cromwell Press Ltd, Wiltshire.

Contents

Series Introduction
The Discourse Power Resistance Series: a Reflection iv
Elizabeth Atkinson

Introduction ix
Jerome Satterthwaite

1   The Elephant in the Living Room: or extending the 1
    conversation about the politics of evidence
    Norman K. Denzin

2   Degrees of Denial: as global heating happens should we 17
    be educating for sustainable development or sustainable
    contraction?
    David Selby

3   Vulnerability – Analytical Concept or Rhetorical Idiom? 35
    Frank Furedi

4   Risky Research or Researching Risk: 51
    the role of ethics review
    Pat Sikes and Heather Piper

5   Whose Truth? Whose (Who's In) Power? International 67
    development, qualitative methodologies and science in
    Central America
    Susan Heald

6   'A Better Place to Live': School history textbooks, 83
    nationalist fantasies, and the incarcerating banality of
    white supremacy
    Ken Montgomery

7   Narrative Research, Narrative Capital, Narrative Capability 99
    Michael Watts

v

8   Speaking Truth to Power: Edward Said and the work of   113
    the intellectual
    Fazal Rizvi

9   Blaspheming Self-Image: the reinterpretation of African   127
    American identity and other disruptions of contemporary
    master narratives
    James Haywood Rolling, Jr.

10 The 'R' Word: voicing race as a critical problem and not   143
    just a problem of practice
    Paul Warmington

Authors' biographies   159

Index   163

The Discourse Power Resistance Series: a Reflection

ELIZABETH ATKINSON

The *Discourse Power Resistance* series offers radical new perspectives on educational research, theory, policy and practice for all those in education – students, teachers, trainers, lecturers, researchers, managers and policy makers – who are caught up in the contemporary matrix of globalised, marketised, neo-liberal education and its corrollaries: centralised educational control, external and internal policing by policy makers, managers and co-practitioners and the demands of the audit-and-output society.

In my introduction to the third volume in this series, *Educational Counter-Cultures: Confrontations, images, vision* (2004) I wrote, 'This book is a song of resistance'. This description speaks for the whole DPR series. These books, which arise from the international *Discourse Power Resistance* conferences, take key themes out into the educational world: the books, the conferences and the debate they have engendered have generated an academic and political movement which reaches beyond the boundaries of nations and disciplines, bringing together powerful voices from around the world in resistance to the marketised control and ideological policing of education.

These voices include some of the most esteemed researchers in their fields, but the book series is also about letting subaltern voices be heard: through the words of contributors from many nations, new insights are offered from those who are normally marginalised, silenced and powerless. A key feature of these voices is that they are multiple, separate and sometimes dissonant: DPR does not promote single, easy solutions, but offers a kaleidoscope of perspectives on things as they are; and a host of new imaginaries for things as they might be.

DPR has developed an increasingly strong presence in the international research community since its first conference in 2002, and now encompasses at its core a collaboration between the original DPR team at the University of Plymouth, the Education and Social Research Institute at Manchester Metropolitan University and the International Association of Qualitative Inquiry led by Norman Denzin at the University of Illinois at Urbana-Champaign. It has provided a crucial forum for radical critique of contemporary trends in education, maintaining a steady interrogation of the comfort zone of the educational establishment in the light of increasingly draconian control of educational research and practice. Both the conferences and the book series demonstrate the power of research as a subversive activity, research as a way of speaking truth to power (to echo the themes of two recent conferences), maintaining that essential role of the researcher as an independent voice of critique at a time when we are all too easily drawn into régimes of control and practices of compliance.

Other titles in the series

Satterthwaite, J, Atkinson, E and Gale, K (eds) (2003) *Discourse, Power, Resistance: Challenging the Rhetoric of Contemporary Education.* Stoke-on-Trent: Trentham

Satterthwaite, J, Atkinson, E and Martin, M (eds) (2004) *The Disciplining of Education: New Languages of Power and Resistance.* Stoke-on-Trent: Trentham

Satterthwaite, J, Atkinson, E and Martin, W (eds) (2004) *Educational Counter-Cultures: Confrontations, Images, Vision.* Stoke-on-Trent: Trentham

Satterthwaite, J, and Atkinson, E (eds) (2005) *Discourses of Education in the Age of New Imperialism.* Stoke-on-Trent: Trentham

Satterthwaite, J, Martin, W and Roberts, L (eds) (2006) *Discourse, Resistance and Identity Formation.* Stoke-on-Trent: Trentham

Introduction

JEROME SATTERTHWAITE

This book is about truth and power and how they are related. We show that everywhere and always power is involved in the project of discovering and constructing truths and in the telling of those truths. We show that power works through culture: that cultures are saturated with power and that powerful cultures work to overwhelm the less powerful. We show that knowledge – what it is, how it is brought forward and published – is always political.

These are not new ideas. In 2004 Patti Lather (Satterthwaite *et al*, 2004: 24) commented that

> With randomised field trials ... or randomised control trials ... now specified by Congress ever more frequently in effectiveness studies of federally funded programmes, the design and application of educational research has become a partisan tool, in much the same way as standardised tests have functioned for almost two decades.

Peter McLaren put it more brutally (Satterthwaite *et al*: 2005: 7): '...truth is whatever it needs to be to secure the strategic interests of the US.' McLaren was writing in an ugly mood because what was at stake seemed to him urgent: that truth-telling should not be banished from the agora, the place of public assembly and debate. This book opens on that issue, with Norman Denzin's analysis of the politics of evidence. Denzin shows that by insisting on the methods and methodology of quantitative inquiry a narrowly restricted view of what counts as knowledge is imposed on research. This matters because what can be captured by these methods may or may not be factual, but will assuredly not be truthful. At least in the social sciences and humanities, and probably in the natural sciences too, truth is not disclosed merely through an assemblage of statements of fact.

Quantitative methods supply the evidence within a meagre epistemology; its definitions are exposed by Denzin as restricting knowledge to the set of two-dimensional objective statements about the social world. What is at work behind the scenes in this account of knowledge as the accumulation of quantifiable facts? Why, on this view, does anything not measurable, not quantifiable, fall short of knowledge – if you can't count it, it doesn't count? Two possible accounts are suggested throughout the discussions in this book.

The first is the hard-headed businessman's preference for the useful knowledge which has routinely been approved as suitable for the working classes, a preference articulated with shocking brutality when Dr Verwoerd, then South Africa's minister of 'Native Affairs', laid down in the Bantu Education Act (1953) that black Africans 'should be educated for their opportunities in life' and that there was no place for them in South African society 'above the level of certain forms of labour'. This is education intended for an inferior social group, and has normally been coupled with concern for the morals of that group (see Golby, 1986) for the views of Samuel Smiles (pp.106-112), John Stuart Mill (pp.263-266) and William Morris (pp.233-4).

This account of knowledge and of the education that sets out to provide it is identified and criticised in every chapter of this book. We show that this is an epistemology close coupled with the need for certainty, leading to the view that only what is certain can be known, so that knowledge can be founded on the rock of fact rather than the shifting sand of more complex and nuanced understanding. Gender is relevant here: in this account of knowledge there is apparent a recrudescence of that manly distaste for the personal and the private that informed the public school ethos of the 19th Century. On this view the personal is taboo – both sacred and accursed – because to look into the self is to explore darkness, the depth below the surface. There is acute uneasiness about where this may lead us; and this fear promotes, paradoxically for an epistemology that sets out to stick to the facts, the habit of deception: a refusal to come clean. There are thoughts and feelings that are not allowed, that we will not tell anyone else because we will not acknowledge them ourselves. In this process of denial the truth is suppressed.

God is closely associated with the notion of truth as a shallow matter of facts. It is interesting that concern for scientific objectivity goes together with the rise of religious fundamentalism (Hedges, 2007; for a calmer assessment of the threat from US Christian Fundamentalism, see the review by Nicholas Guyatt (LRB, 15.11.07). The connection is that 'God's eye' (to which Denzin refers) sees, and therefore God knows, everything for certain. God is not misled by seeing less than the whole picture; nor is his perception skewed by cultural influences, which he rises above, being detached from any culture. This being so, he gets things right in an absolute sense, both as regards matters of fact and matters of value. Christian believers who have access to his mind bypass all the potential troublesome distractions and patchiness of our earth-bound vision, and encounter Truth in all its naked perfection. This enables them, by extension, to recognise Error in all its filthy degradation. What is lacking here, as Denzin demonstrates, is self-criticism. The result is systematic distortion and partiality, together with the unreflective mistrust of alternative views and the methodologies that inform them.

This book is published at a time when issues about what can be known and how we can know it are extremely urgent, because our world is heating up. Energy that took sixty million years to store is taking us some two centuries to release, flash heating our world and leading to catastrophic consequences. This is something we know; and we know it through empirical observation and the gathering of statistics – precisely the procedures adopted by quantitative research. Whether the world is heating up or not is a matter of careful observation; what to do about it requires wisdom and political will – knowledge of an altogether different kind (Monbiot, 2006; Lynas, 2007). David Selby shows how the framework of our contemporary epistemology, together with its content, assumptions, methods and methodologies and their associated value-systems, have combined to lead inevitably to crisis. He argues for a return to holistic knowledge: that whole-person, whole-society, whole-world embrace in which the insights of the poets, mystics and lovers are brought together with the findings of empirical science. This is not moist sentimentality; it is the hard, realistic prescription of the minimum required for the continuance on this planet of life as we know it. Selby's argument is plain: since it is human agency, informed by a shallow view of what is valuable, that is bringing about the devastation of the planet, it will be only through a radical shift in human understanding that the damage can be stopped.

How far removed such radical change is from the real-life practice and ideology of contemporary decision-making is brought out in Frank Furedi's analysis – in effect a case-study of the trivialisation at work in professional discourse – of the concept of vulnerability. Furedi traces the emergence and steady growth of the use of this term as a label for a range of social groups and individuals, perceived and categorised as victims or potential victims. Furedi writes: 'What we characterise as the rhetoric of vulnerability works as a rhetorical idiom that situates particular individuals and groups and their experience, within a context of powerlessness and lack of agency'. We make groups vulnerable so that we can elicit sympathy for them, do things for them and speak up on their behalf. Members of these 'vulnerable' groups are inhibited from taking action for themselves. Resourcefulness on their part is at odds with the perception of them from outside the group; and members of the group are easily coaxed into a similar understanding of themselves and their situations, and encouraged to become receptive to a range of therapeutic interventions on their behalf. Perceived as vulnerable by professionals and other privileged commentators, members of these groups learn to accept this view of themselves constructed from expert outsiders, and come to suppose that the experts know and understand them better than they know themselves. They learn the codes and behaviour associated with membership of a vulnerable group and adopt the expectations appropriate to victims.

Power is clearly at work in the categorisation of individuals or groups as vulnerable. Having been constructed as victims, the members of the 'vulnerable' group do indeed become victims, but now of the care and concern of the experts who classified them as such. We are reminded of Foucault, whose writing is pervaded by the recognition that professionals of all kinds need vulnerable groups, just as the police need criminals. Effectively, to characterise a group as vulnerable is to lay claim to a specialism – a branch of expert, more or less arcane, knowledge – and to construct the individual or group as vulnerable in the sense of having a peculiar need which only this expertise can meet. This is a self-serving and shallow understanding, diminishing the whole person or social group who are the subject of this categorisation: all that need be known about them is their vulnerability, variously defined to meet the experts' needs.

A particularly disturbing account, raising acutely and painfully the issues of talking truth and confronting power, is the chapter by Heather Piper and Pat Sikes about their research into allegations of sexual abuse. Piper and Sikes understand their project as relating to two groups, either or both of whom may be construed as vulnerable. On the one hand there are school children who have accused school teachers of abusing them; on the other are teachers, the subject of these accusations. For reasons they make clear, the authors decided to restrict their research to the group of teachers and to look at the issues raised by becoming the subject of an accusation of this kind. It was no part of the authors' project to determine the truth or falsehood of the allegations: they are not judges but academic researchers. Their project was to examine the impact of such allegations on the teachers' careers and reputations, their standing amongst colleagues, pupils and parents and in their families and communities, their health, their colleagues and managers, their perceptions of themselves and other aspects of the impact upon them of being accused of sexual abuse.

The chapter recounts and reflects upon the authors' experiences of seeking approval from Ethics Committees and applying for funding. The authors scrupulously preserve the anonymity of individuals and groups who considered and found fault with their submissions. But their story speaks for itself: here is an example of the intervention of powerful groups – committees with the power to withhold approval, funding bodies with the power to withhold funding – advised by experts, at least one of whom had serious misgivings about her fitness to form an unbiased opinion. These groups acted over a period of some considerable time to delay and frustrate a serious, topical and urgent issue of social justice. The issue of vulnerability as Furedi analyses it dominates the procedures Piper and Sikes describe; but this is partial vulnerability, applied to construct the children as victims, and the adults as their presumed abusers. At a secondary level there were concerns that institutions might themselves be vulnerable – to litigation. It is worth noting one further ironic detail: the decision to publish this chapter was delayed until one of the experts involved was finally satisfied that the making public of her opinions would not make her a victim – vulnerable to disrespect.

We have noted the anxieties surrounding the probing involved in qualitative research. It seems there is a deep-down problem in talking truth. When the subject has been accorded a quasi-sacred status, it becomes unspeakable. Furedi shows that 'the vulnerable' have been given this status; Piper and Sikes' chapter shows what the consequences are. 'The vulnerable' become a more or less sacrosanct group, set apart, their well-being accorded a special status and their testimony privileged, placed above and beyond the reach of criticism. To criticise the vulnerable is to compromise their status as untouchable. Piper and Sikes' refusal of this irrationality allows them to ask what is going on and to question whether those accused of abuse may themselves be a vulnerable group. But in the mind-set Furedi has analysed, this question is blasphemous and must not be pursued. So their research is hindered and funding withheld.

Heather Piper and Pat Sikes give an account of research which powerful groups appear anxious to obstruct. Susan Heald recounts a similar experience, but in her case it was not only the representatives of the academy who were uneasy about her work. The students themselves, the group whose interests she set out to serve, distanced themselves from her project, preferring the approach and ideology of the master group whose attitudes Heald had set out to challenge. Her aim was to talk with, rather than to, colleagues in Central American universities. Instead, she found herself caught up in a web of suspicions and misunderstandings, where barriers of language and culture and unspoken assumptions of cultural superiority gave her no room to manoeuvre. Heald found herself unable to work in this system, where the friendship and solidarity amongst equals, which she insists is a precondition of serious learning together, was impossible. Her question is one of the challenges of this book: is it the case that identity politics brings research to a halt, and that, given what she calls *the imperial gestures of dominant knowledge-making practices*, we can, in the end, only know ourselves – the white, heterosexual middle classes? It is a question raised again by Ken Montgomery. He sees Canadian educators – specifically the authors and authorisers of contemporary History textbooks – unconsciously colluding in the replication of racist thinking in their celebration of Canada as a multicultural utopia. Beneath the euphoria he detects all the old bigotry at work, evidencing 'the embeddedness of racism within the banal structures and taken-for-granted experiences that organise life in a modern racial state'.

Michael Watts looks at issues similar to those raised by Susan Heald, but he takes a more sanguine view. Heald, rightly, feels at a loss, confronted by a dogmatic refusal to question the status of the dominant culture and its discursive formations – a dogmatism shared by managers, colleagues and students, who are agreed that there is only one valid knowledge and one valid way of articulating it, acquiescing in and, indeed, celebrating the cultural imperialism encoded in this view. Watts, in a context less rigidly determined by assumptions of cultural superiority, argues for a pedagogy of cultural coaching. His players are seen as fully developed in the narrative skills of their own idiom but correspondingly disadvantaged in another more dominant discourse. The researcher acts as coach, recognising the narrative competence of these players but working alongside them in what is in effect an exercise in cultural – and therefore narrative – translation. The coach is no better a player in this game: along with Heald, Watts insists that there is no reach-me-down superiority implicit in the stance of narrative enabler. The work of bringing forward the narrative competence of disadvantaged groups is done by researcher and narrators working alongside one another in a relationship of mutual exchange.

One formulation of the question central to this book might be: *Who can speak, how, under what conditions, and with what consequences – and with what purpose?* This is the question asked by Fazal Rizvi. It is the question at the heart of the writing and speaking of Edward Said, whose work may be seen as a lifelong interrogation of the uneasiness, and strength, of being positioned as an outsider to a dominant culture. Said belongs everywhere and nowhere: a brilliant, passionate interpreter of Western European culture who was himself non-European, an outstanding academic with a critical view of the preoccupations of the academy, his work is fundamental to our understanding of cultural imperialism and the difficulties for the outsider of speaking truth to power. Rizvi celebrates with Said the role of the outsider, whose cultural distance is at once a problem and a strength; but he notes also how easily outsiders may come to adopt the status of refugees, unwilling to speak out, afraid of being identified as alien, withholding their critique in awkward silences, whispering their truths only to one another as confidential asides.

For Paul Warmington, as for Ken Montgomery, race is central and pervasive: 'normal, non-aberrant, non-exotic' in the everyday experience of our social lives, which are 'sinewed by race practices'. Race is everywhere inscribed in the theory and practice of everyday life; it is so thoroughly integrated into the culture that we do not recognise it, and are disconcerted when the claim is made that our everyday experience is saturated with racialised assumptions. We want and need to suppose that race is a category that may be applied to attitudes and behaviour elsewhere, beyond the pale of our own normal experience and the world view through which that experience is interpreted. The suppression of race reaches its limit in the refusal of whites to recognise themselves as belonging to any race at all: race is then a category of otherness. 'We are not yet post-racial', Warmington concludes; 'for that reason, the race concept must be subject to constant interrogation'.

James Rolling does this; but perhaps 'interrogation' is too poised a word for the intensity of the grief and anger, the 'descent into chaos and loss' of his exploration of the experience of being an African American in a culture still saturated with racism. Rolling repositions himself through opposition – to his father and to 'the modernist master narratives that would constrain the indecorous splatter of our inquiry' – that is, to the methodology of quantitative inquiry. These are the sources of authority he opposes. (We are reminded of Patti Lather's title: 'This *IS* your father's paradigm [Lather, 2004: 21].) It is all about identity, names and naming: the names put upon him by the dominant group, his own defiant un-naming and re-naming of himself. Rolling gives himself a voice and names himself. And he gives voice to and names the group where he belongs: 'I give voice to myself. I give voice to the collective'. But also, he un-names: 'I act to un-name all other Juniors in the act of un-naming myself. Those unborn. Those postmortem. Those unfathered. This is, after all, a collective story'.

This book brings together the testimony of a group of international scholars on the issue of talking truth and confronting power. They are writing about the difficulty, but also about the urgent need, of talking truth and confronting power.

References

Bantu Education Act (1953) http://www.photius.com/countries/south_africa/society/south_africa_society_the_bantu_education_~2456.html

Golby, J (ed) (1986) *Culture and Society and Britain 1850-1890: a source book of contemporary writings.* Oxford: Oxford University Press

Guyatt, N (2007) Blackberry Apocalypse. *London Review of Books* 15.11.207

Hedges, C (2007) *American Fascists: the Christian Right and the War on America.* London: Vintage

Lather, P (2004) Foucauldian scientificity: rethinking the nexus of qualitative research and educational policy analysis. *International Journal of Qualitative Studies in Education* 19(6) p783-792

Lynas, M (2007) *Six Degrees: our future on a hotter planet.* London: Fourth Estate

Monbiot, G (2006) *Heat: how we can stop the planet burning.* London: Penguin

Satterthwaite, J, and Atkinson, E (eds) (2005) *Discourses of Education in the Age of New Imperialism.* Stoke-on-Trent: Trentham

Satterthwaite, J, Atkinson, E and Martin, M (eds) (2004) *The Disciplining of Education: New Languages of Power and Resistance.* Stoke-on-Trent: Trentham

1

The Elephant in the Living Room: or extending the conversation about the politics of evidence

NORMAN K. DENZIN

Speaker One: (American Education Research Association – AERA spokesperson– off-stage):

> As part of AERA's broader educational mission to advance high-quality research in education and to foster excellence in reporting on empirical research, the Association commends use of these standards in the training and preparation of researchers in publishing research. (AERA, 2006:2)

Speaker Two: (Campbell Methods Group spokesperson – off-stage):

> Members of the Methods Group are exploring ... in the context of existing Cochrane and Campbell systematic reviews ... whether only qualitative research within RCTs should be included. (Briggs, 2006: 2)

Prologue

Qualitative researchers are caught in the middle of a global conversation concerning standards and guidelines for conducting and evaluating qualitative inquiry. This conversation turns on issues surrounding the politics and ethics of evidence, and the value of qualitative work in addressing matters of equity and social justice (Lather, 2004: 789).

Within the global audit culture proposals concerning the use of Cochrane and Campbell criteria,[1] experimental methodologies, randomised clinical trials, quantitative metrics, citation analyses, shared data bases, journal impact factors, rigid notions of accountability, data transparency, warrantablity, rigorous peer-review evaluation scales and fixed formats for scientific articles now compete, fighting to gain ascendancy in the evidence-quality-standards discourse (Thomas, 2004, 2006: 21; NRC, 2002: 47; Feuer, Towne and Shavelson, 2002).

Using a multi-voiced performance text format[2], I want to read the controversies surrounding this discourse within a critical pedagogical framework (Denzin, 2003). I hope to chart a path of resistance for qualitative researchers. I seek a performance model of qualitative inquiry that enacts an ethic based on feminist, communitarian assumptions. This commitment opens the space for a discussion of ethics, science, causality, trust and a reiteration of moral and ethical criteria for judging qualitative research (Denzin, 2003; Denzin, Lincoln and Giardina, 2006; Denzin, 2007).

Act One: The Elephant in the Living Room
Scene One: Whose room is it anyway?

Speaker One: Jan Morse (2006, [paraphrase]):

> Indeed, qualitative inquiry falls off the positivist grid. Why, it barely earns a Grade of C- on the Cochrane scale! It gets worse! It receives the 'does not meet evidence standard' on the 'What Works Clearinghouse' (WWC) Scale. (Morse, 2006: 396; Cheek, 2005, 2006)

Speakers One and Two: Feuer, Towne and Shavelson (2002, [paraphrase]):

> We strongly oppose blunt federal mandates that reduce scientific inquiry to one method ... But it is time for the field to move beyond particularised views and focus on building a core of norms and practices that emphasise shared scientific principles. (p.8)

Speaker One: Spokesperson, National Centre for the Dissemination of Disability Research, 2007:

> [paraphrase]): We need criteria for comparing research methods and research evidence, we need terms like credibility (internal vali-

dity), transferability (external validity), dependability (reliability), confirmability (objectivity).

Like an elephant in the living room, the evidence-based model is an intruder whose presence can no longer be ignored.

Two Other Elephants

The elephant wears at least two garments, the cloak of evidence-based inquiry, and the disguises of mix-methods research. The mix-methods disguise invites two initiatives. The first involves the production of systematic reviews that incorporate qualitative research into meta-analyses (Dixon-Woods, *et al*, 2006). The second initiative revisits the concept of triangulation and mixed-methods, asking how qualitative and quantitative methods can be made to work together (Ellis, *et al*, 2000).

There are problems with both disguises. Meta-analyses of published articles hardly count as qualitative research in any sense of the word. The return to mix-methods inquiry fails to address the incommensurability issue – the two paradigms are in contradiction and cannot be made to fit together (Smith and Hodkinson, 2005: 922-24).[3]

Scene Two: Whose Criteria, Whose Standards?

Extending Smith and Deemer (2000), within the qualitative inquiry community there are three basic positions on the issue of evaluative criteria: foundational, quasi-foundational and non-foundational (see also Spencer, *et al*, 2003: 39; Creswell, 2007: 203-220; Guba and Lincoln, 2005, 1989; Lincoln and Guba, 1985). Those who think in terms of a foundational epistemology apply the same criteria to qualitative research as are employed in quantitative inquiry, contending that as there is nothing special about qualitative research that demands a special set of evaluative criteria, research is research, quantitative or qualitative. All research should conform to a set of shared criteria. In contrast, quasi-foundationalists contend that a set of criteria unique to qualitative research needs to be developed. Non-foundationalists argue that the injunction to pursue knowledge cannot be given epistemologically; rather the injunction is moral and political.

Speakers One and Two: Smith and Deemer (2000, paraphrased):

The God's-eye view is no longer a realisable hope ... any discussion of criteria for judging social and educational inquiry must confront the issue of relativism. (p.877)

Speaker Two: Harry Torrance (2006: 127):

This new orthodoxy seems perversely and wilfully, ignorant of many decades of debate over whether, and if so in what ways we can conduct enquiry and build knowledge in the social sciences.

Speaker One: Ian Stronach (2006: 758):

This current dispute between qualitative and quantitative research is international, acrimonious, and there are elements of state-sponsored support in the West for a return to a kind of neopositivist quantitative inquiry.

Speaker Two: Martyn Hammersley (2005: 4 paraphrase):

We probably need to invent a ... myth that we too have clear-cut guidelines and criteria; maybe not randomised control trials, but we have our criteria!

Speakers One and Two: Discourse, Power Resistance Group (paraphrase):

Listen, we conceptualise research as subversive activity, none of this consensual stuff, searching for common ground and all that! We endorse work that unsettles, challenges and contests existing social and educational formations, work that resists those narrowly defined quantitative forms of inquiry that are favoured by those neoconservative policy-makers with their federal and private funding bodies.

Scene Three: The Politics of Evidence

Evidence is never morally or ethically neutral. But, paraphrasing Morse, who quotes Larner (2004: 20), the politics and political economy of evidence is not a question of evidence or no evidence. It is rather a question of who has the power to control the definition of evidence. Clearly, the politics of evidence cannot be separated from the ethics of evidence.

Act Two: State and discipline sponsored epistemologies
Scene One: Multiple Realities

This ethical, epistemological and political discourse is historically and politically situated. It plays out differently in each national context[4] (see Atkinson and Delamont, 2006; Cheek, 2006; Morse, 2006; Gilgun, 2006; Preissle, 2006). In the United States, the UK, Continental Europe, (Atkinson and Delamont, 2006), New Zealand and Australia (Cheek, 2005, 2006) the conversation criss-crosses audit cultures, indigenous cultures, disciplines, paradigms and epistemologies, as well as decolonising initiatives. There is not a single discourse. In the postpositivist American community, there are multiple conversations competing for attention. I focus here on just one, the 2006 standards for reporting adopted by the American Education Research Association (AERA) which explicitly addresses standards for qualitative research, some of which are contained in documents prepared by members of the Cochrane Qualitative Methods Group (Briggs, 2006).[5]

Scene Two: AERA and Peer Reviews

The AERA recommends that scholarly societies develop explicit ethical standards for data sharing, with the proviso that confidentiality be maintained. (In the post America 9/11 Patriot Act culture), data collected by any scientist are no longer confidential.) Data sharing enables re-analyses and replications. In an evidence-based, Cochrane-Campbell environment, systematic meta-analyses of existing data sets become critical. These projects rely on access to such information. They presume the ability to assemble reliable, valid, systematic evidence-based reviews. In order for these reviews to be written, journals must require authors to make relevant data available to other researchers as a condition of publication, and to ensure that appropriate ethical standards have been upheld. If this is done, members of the Cochrane-Campbell Collaboration have immediate access to the materials their meta-analyses require. These analyses and data bases become on-line commodities, packaged and sold, courtesy of Wiley-Interscience, publishers.

There are fundamental flaws with this group of recommendations. Giving little justification, they require that a new set of procedures be implemented, from peer reviews of published works to new require-

5

ments for journal editors.[6] They implement only one methodology. They presume that objective reviewers use objective criteria to produce objective peer-reviews. This is problematic: there are no objective reviewers, and no objective criteria. Hence the objective peer-review is a fiction, a necessary myth for this form of science. Just because there are so-called peer reviews of scientific work, this 'does not mean that the reviews are themselves a scientific process' (Knoll, 1990: 31).

Scene Three: Guidelines for Performing Data

The AERA 2006 guidelines for reporting on empirical social science research are also intended to foster excellence in the production of high quality research. Two global standards are offered, warrantability and transparency[7] (AERA, 2006: 2). Reports of research should be warranted, that is, supported by adequate evidence, which would be credible (internal validity) and should be adequate to justify conclusions. Reports should be transparent, making explicit the logic of inquiry used in the project.[8] This method should produce data that have external validity, reliability and confirmability or objectivity. Like the NRC guidelines, these standards are to be used by peer-reviewers, research scholars, journal publishers and in graduate education programmes where researchers are trained. There is extensive discussion of quantitative procedures (*ibid*: 6-10), although there is little attention given to how data are turned into evidence and into shareable data-banks. Data are not silent. Data are commodities, data are performative, data are not passive. When the report moves to qualitative methods the matter of trust surfaces. Qualitative inquiry is presented as an iterative process: the researcher develops claims, interpretations, seeking confirming and disconfirming evidence in the data. Analysis ceases when researchers are satisfied and can provide evidence that their data interpretations meaningfully characterise the data analysed.

Trust

Trust is not a topic in the discussion of quantitative methods. Trust is an issue for qualitative researchers. The report is explicit:

Speaker One: AERA:

> It is the researcher's responsibility to show the reader that the report can be trusted. This begins with the description of the evidence, the data, and the analysis supporting each interpretive claim. When the evidence does not converge ... critical examination of the ... perspectives of the researcher, of how these might have influenced the collection and analysis of evidence, and of how they were challenged during the course of data collection and analysis, is an important element in enhancing the warrant of each claim (p.11).

Narrator:

> Here is the heart of the matter. The perspective of the qualitative researcher can influence the collection of evidence in such a way as to introduce a lack of trust into the research process. This presence potentially undermines the credibility and warrantability of the report.

Speaker Two:

> They used to call this internal validity; now it's trust!

With a responsible use of scientific tools, threats to trust (transparency) can be overcome. Trust is increased by highlighting the evidence and alternative interpretations that serve as a warrant for each claim, by providing contextual commentary on each claim. When generalisations extend beyond a specific case, researchers must clearly indicate the sampling frame, population, individuals, contexts, activities and domains to which the generalisations are intended to apply (external validity). The logic supporting such generalisations must be made clear.

A sleight of hand is at work in the AERA recommendations. The intent of the report is now clear. Two things are going on at once: a familiar pattern. Qualitative research is down-graded to the status of a marginal, second-class science. Since it lacks trustworthiness, it can be used for discovery purposes, but not for the real work of science, which is verification. Only under the most rigorous of circumstances can qualitative research exhibit the qualities that would make it scientific, and even then trust will be an issue. Trust becomes a proxy for quality and transparency; warranted evidence functions as a proxy for objectivity.

Scene Four: Re-Reading Trust and Ethics

Trust in this discourse re-surfaces as a proxy for more than quality. It spills over to the researcher who does research that lacks trust. Untrustworthy persons lie, misrepresent, cheat, engage in fraud, alter documents. They are not governed by measurement and statistical procedures that are objective and free of bias. They may not be shady characters, they may be well-intended, gifted actors, poets, fiction writers, performers, but they are not scientists! Qualitative researchers are not to be trusted because their standpoints can influence what they study, and report. Somehow quantitative researchers are freed from these influences. This of course is a sham!

Speaker One:

> But isn't it the quantitative scientists who are being charged with fraud, with misrepresenting their data? Who says qualitative researchers do this?

Speaker Two:

> Let me help you here. You see many qualitative researchers don't have data and findings, tables and charts, statistics and numbers. We have stories, narratives, excerpts from interviews. We perform our interpretations and invite audiences to experience these performances, to live their way into the scenes, moments and lives we are writing and talking about. Our data can't be fudged, mis-represented, altered or distorted, because our data are life experiences. They are ethno-dramas.

It seems that the qualitative community is hemmed in from all sides. But before this judgment is accepted, the 'for whom' question must be asked (Cheek, 2006). AERA and Strategic Business Research (SBR) umbrellas are too small. We need a larger tent.

Act Three: The Qualitative Inquiry Community
Scene One: Trouble at Home

We must resist the pressures for a single gold standard, even as we endorse conversations about evidence, inquiry and empirically warranted conclusions (Lincoln and Cannella, 2004; Schwandt, 2006: 808). We cannot let one group define the key terms in the conversation. To do this is to allow the SBR group to define the moral and epistemological ground that we stand on. Neither they, nor the government own the word 'science'. Over forty years ago Habermas (1972) anticipated this.

Speakers One and Two: Habermas (paraphrase), see also Smith and Hodkinson (2005: 930):

> The link between empiricism, positivism and the global audit culture is not accidental and it is more than just technical. Such technical approaches ... make radical critiques much more difficult to mount ... they render largely invisible partisan approaches to research under the politically useful pretence that judgments are about objective quality only. In the process human needs and human rights are trampled upon. (1972: 22; 2006: 193)

Speaker One: Bourdieu (1998: 90):

> The technocrats, and empiricists are hand in glove with reason and the universal ... More and more rational, scientific technical justifications, always in the name of objectivity, are relied upon. In this way the audit culture perpetuates itself.

There is more than one version of disciplined, rigorous inquiry: counter-science, little science, unruly science, practical science; and such inquiry need not go by the name of science. We must have a model of disciplined, rigorous, thoughtful, reflective inquiry, a 'post-interpretivism that seeks meaning but less innocently, that seeks liberation but less naively, and that ... reaches toward understanding, transformation and justice' (Preissle, 2006: 692; St. Pierre and Rouleston, 2006; Eisenhart, 2006).

Speaker Two: Patti Lather, (paraphrase):

> The commitment to disciplined inquiry opens the space for a disciplined inquiry that matters, applied qualitative research ... that can engage strategically with the limits and the possibilities of the uses of research for social policy. (Lather, 2004: 787)

Scene Two: A New Terrain, Trouble with the Elephant
Narrator:

> Let's return to the elephant in the living room. Consider the parable of the blind men and the elephant.

Speaker One: (Lillian Quigley, from *The Blind Men and the Elephant* (1959/1996):

In an ancient fable six blind men visit the palace of the Rajah and encounter an elephant for the first time. Each touches the elephant, and announces his discovery. The first blind person touches the side of the elephant and reports that it feels like a wall. The second touches the trunk and says an elephant is like a snake. The third man touches the tusk and says an elephant is like a spear. The fourth person touches a leg and says it feels like a tree. The fifth man touches an ear and says it must be a fan, while the sixth man touches the tail and says how thin it is: an elephant is like a rope.

Speaker Two:

The Rajah: Each of you touched only one part of the elephant. You must put all the parts together to find out what an elephant is like.

Speaker One:

Blind men in unison: Oh my, each of us knows only a part. How do we put the parts together?

Speaker Two:

Philosopher: This fable has been used to make two points. The first is that every perspective represents just a part of a larger truth: each one has only a piece of the truth. The second is that, as sceptics hold, cultural biases have so seriously blinded us that we can never see the true nature of things.

Speaker One:

Second Philosopher: What if the elephant speaks? If so we have a new standard for judging who the elephant is.

Speaker Two:

Second Sceptic: What if we are all like blind persons, fumbling around in the world searching for answers to life's deepest questions? Occasionally we stumble upon something we can call a truth, but most of the time we are confused.

There are multiple versions of the elephant in this parable, and multiple lessons.

Truth One: The elephant is not one thing. If we call SBR the elephant, then according to the parable, we can each know only our version of SBR. For SBR advocates, the elephant is two things, an all-knowing being who speaks to us, and a way of knowing that produces truths about life.

Truth Two: For sceptics, we are like the blind persons in the parable. We only see partial truths. There is no God's view of the totality.

Truth Three: Our methodological and moral biases have so seriously blinded us that we can never understand another person's position. Even if the elephant called SBR speaks, our biases may prohibit us for hearing what she says. In turn, her biases prevent her from hearing what we say.

Truth Four: If we are all blind, if there is no God, and if there are multiple versions of the elephant then we are all fumbling around in the world just doing the best we can.

Scene Three: Two Other Versions of the Elephant

This is the blind person's version of the elephant. There are at least two other versions, 2. 1 and 2 .2. Both versions follow from another fable. Now the elephant refers to a painfully problematic situation, thing or person in one's life space. Rather than confront the thing, and make changes, persons find that it is easier to engage in denial, to act as if the elephant isn't in the room. This can be unhealthy, because the thing may be destructive. It can produce co-dependency: we come to need the negative presence of the elephant in order to feel good about ourselves.

This cuts two ways at once. In Fable 2.1 SBR advocates treating qualitative research as if it were an elephant in their living room. They have ignored our traditions, our values, our methodologies; they have not read our journals. They have not even engaged with our discourses about SBR. Like the six blind men, they have acted as if they could create us in their own eye. They say we produce findings that cannot be trusted; we are radical relativists, we think anything goes. Acting like the Rajah, thinking they are like God, they dismiss us when we tell them they only know one version of who we are. When we tell them their biases prevent them from understanding what we do they assert that we are wrong and they are right.

In Fable 2.2 the elephant is located in our living room. With notable exceptions, we have tried to ignore this presence. Denial has fed co-dependency. We need the negative presence of SBR to define who we are. For example, we have not taken up the challenge of educating policy-makers better and showing them how qualitative research and our views of practical science, interpretation and performance ethics can positively contribute to projects embodying restorative justice, equity and better schooling (Stanfield, 2006; Preissle, 2006). We have not engaged policy-makers in a dialogue about alternative ways of judging and evaluating quality research; nor have we engaged SBR advocates in a dialogue about these same issues (but see St. Pierre and Raulson, 2006); and, they have often declined the invitation to join us in a conversation. As a consequence, we have let the SBR elephant set the terms of the conversation.

If we are to move forward positively we have to get beyond Fable 2. 2, beyond elephants, blind persons and structures of denial. We must create a new narrative, a narrative of passion and commitment, a narrative which teaches others that ways of knowing are always already moral and political. This narrative will allow us to put the elephant in proper perspective. Here are the certain things we can build our new fable around:

1. We have an ample supply of methodological rules and inter-pretive guidelines.

2. They are open to change and to differing interpretation, and this is how it should be.

3. There is no longer a single gold standard for qualitative work.

4. We value open-peer reviews in our journals.

5. Our empirical materials are performative. They are not commodi-ties to be bought, sold and consumed.

6. Our feminist, communitarian ethics are not governed by IRBs.

7. Our science is open-ended, unruly, disruptive. (MacLure, 2006; Stronach, *et al* 2007: 197)

8. Inquiry is always political and moral.

9. Objectivity and evidence are political and ethical terms.

We live in a depressing historical moment: violent spaces, unending wars against persons of colour, repression, the falsification of evidence, the collapse of critical, democratic discourse; and repressive neo-liberalism, disguised as dispassionate objectivity, prevails. Global efforts to impose a new orthodoxy on critical social science inquiry must be resisted; a hegemonic politics of evidence cannot be allowed. Too much is at stake.

Notes

1   The Cochrane Collaboration (CC) is an international not-for-profit organisation founded in 1993, and named after the British epidemiologist, Archie Cochrane. The collaboration produces and disseminates reviews of healthcare interventions and promotes the use of experimental, evidence-based methods of research. Formed in 1998, also as a non-profit organisation, the International Campbell Collaboration (C2), named after Donald Campbell is intended to do for the social sciences what the Cochrane does for health care: provide access to and summaries of evidence-based studies on the effects of social interventions and educational practices (Lather, 2006: 31). The Campbell Collaboration is affiliated with the American Institute for Research (AIR), a nonpartisan, not for profit behavioural and social science contract research organisation. The C2 reports on experiments and quasi-experiments relating to schooling, delinquency, criminal justice, mental health, welfare, housing and employment. The steering committee for C2 is chaired by Robert Boruch, who is also the Principle Investigator of the What Works Clearinghouse (WWC). The WWC, established in 2002, is administered by the US Department of Education's Institute of Education Science, through a joint venture with the AIR and C2. The WWC collects, screens and identifies studies of effectiveness of educational intervention programmes. Rigorous experimental standards are employed, and studies are placed in one of three categories: meets evidence standards; meets evidence standards with reservations; does not meet evidence standards (see http://w-w-c.org/whoweare/overview.html#ies). There has been a recent move within both collaborations to create protocols for evaluating qualitative research studies (see Briggs, 2006).

2   There are three voices: a narrator and speaker one, and speaker two.

3   Over the past four decades the discourse on triangulation, multiple operationalism, and mix-method models has become quite complex and nuanced. Each decade has taken up triangulation and redefined it to meet perceived needs. The very term triangulation is unsettling, and unruly. It disrupts and threatens the belief that reality in its complexities can ever be fully captured or faithfully represented. Drawing from Saukko (2003), one goal is to bring these different views of triangulation and multiperspectival research into play with one another, 'holding them in creative tension with one another ... 'cultivates multidimensional research and politics' (Saukko, 2003: 32). There is no intention of arriving at a final, correct, enlightened view. The goal of multiple, or critical triangulation is a fully grounded interpretative research project with an egalitarian base. Objective reality will never be captured. In-depth understanding, the use of multiple validities, not a single validity, a commitment to dialogue and strong objectivity is sought in any interpretative study.

4   Thus qualitative research seems to thrive in Great Britain, provided it conforms to an agreed-upon set of criteria (see Atkinson and Delamont, 2006). In contrast, Cheek (2005; 2006) presents quite a different picture from Australia.

5   The common threat that exists between WWC and CCC is The No Child Left Behind (NCLB) and Reading First (Reading.First@ed. Gov) Acts. These acts required a focus on identifying and using scientifically based research in designing and implementing educational programmes (*What Works Clearinghouse.* http://w-w-c.org/whoweare/ overview.html#ies.).

6   The APA has had such a data-sharing policy in effect for 25 years, but less than one-tenth of a percent of available data are actually shared (National Research Council, 2002: 45).

7   Warrantability and transparency are key terms in the new managerialism, which is evidence-based, and audit-driven; that is: policy decisions should be based on evidence

that warrants policy recommendations, and research procedures should be transparently accountable (Hammersley, 2005: 141). Transparency is also a criterion advanced by the Cochrane Qualitative Methods Group (Briggs, 2006).

8 These two reporting standards are then divided into eight general areas: problem formation; design and logic of the study; sources of evidence; measurement and classification; analysis and interpretation; generalisation; ethics in reporting; title, abstract and headings.

References

American Education Research Association (2006) Standards for Reporting on Empirical Social Science Research in AERA publications. www.aera.net/opportunities/?id=1480 (accessed February 2007)

Atkinson, P and Delamont, S (2006) In the roiling smoke: qualitative inquiry and contested fields. *International Journal of Qualitative Studies in Education* 19(6) p747-755

Briggs, J (2006) Cochrane Qualitative Research Methods Group. www.joannabriggs.eduau/cqrmg/role.html (accessed September 2007)

Bourdieu, P (1998) *Practical Reason*. Cambridge: Polity

Cannella, G and Lincoln, Y (2004) Dangerous discourses II: comprehending and countering the redeployment of discourses (and resources) in the generation of liberatory inquiry. *Qualitative Inquiry* 10 (2) p165-174

Cheek, J (2005) The practice and politics of funded qualitative research. In N. Denzin and Y. Lincoln (eds) *Handbook of Qualitative Research*, 3rd edition. Thousand Oaks, Ca: Sage

Cheek, J (2006) What's in a number? Issues in providing evidence of impact and quality of research(ers). *Qualitative Health Research* 16(3) p423-435

Creswell, J (2007) *Qualitative Inquiry and Research Design: choosing among five approaches, 2nd edition*. Thousand Oaks, Ca: Sage

Denzin, N (1997) *Interpretive Ethnography*. Thousand Oaks, Ca: Sage

Denzin, N (2003) *Performance Ethnography: critical pedagogy and the politics of culture*. Thousand Oaks, Ca: Sage

Denzin, N (2007) The secret Downing Street Memo and the politics of truth: a performance text. *Symbolic Interaction*, 30(2) in press

Denzin, N, Lincoln, Y and Giardina, M (2006) Disciplining qualitative research. *International Journal of Qualitative Studies in Education* 19(6) p769-782

Dixon-Woods, M, Bonas, S, Booth, A, Jones, D, Jones, T, Sutton, A, Shaw, R, Smith, J and Young, B (2006) How can systematic reviews incorporate qualitative research? A critical perspective. *Qualitative Research* 6(1) p27-44

Eisenhart, M (2006) Qualitative science in experimental time. *International Journal of Qualitative Studies in Education* 19(6) p697-708

Ellis, C (2000) Creating criteria: an ethnographic short story. *Qualitative Inquiry* 6(2) p273-77

Feuer, M, Towne, L and Shavelson, R (2002) Science, culture, and educational research. *Educational Researcher* 31(8) p 4-14

Gilgun, J (2006) The four cornerstones of qualitative research. *Qualitative Health Research* 16(3) p436-443

Guba, E and Lincoln, Y (1989) *Fourth Generation Evaluation*. Newbury Park, Ca: Sage

Guba, E and Lincoln, Y (2005) Paradigmatic controversies and emerging confluences. In N. Denzin and Y. Lincoln (eds) *Handbook of Qualitative Research, 3rd edition*. Thousand Oaks, Ca: Sage

Habermas, J (1972) *Knowledge and Human Interests, 2nd edition*. London: Heinemann

Hammersley, M (2005) Close encounters of a political kind: the threat from the evidence-based policy-making and practice movement. *Qualitative Researcher,* 1(December) p2-4

Knoll, E (1990) The communities of scientists and journal peer reviews. *JAMA: Journal of the American Medical Association* 263(9) p1330-1332

Larner, G (2004) Family therapy and the politics of evidence. *Journal of Family Therapy* 26(1) p17-39

Lather, P (1993) *Getting Smart: feminist research and pedagogy with/in the postmodern.* New York: Routledge

Lather, P (2004) Foucauldian scientificity: rethinking the nexus of qualitative research and educational policy analysis. *International Journal of Qualitative Studies in Education* 19(6) p783-792

Lincoln, Y and Guba, E (1985) *Naturalistic Inquiry.* Beverly Hill, Ca: Sage

Lincoln, Y and Cannella, G (2004) Dangerous discourses: methodological conservatism and governmental regimes of truth. *Qualitative Inquiry* 10(1) p5-10

MacLure, M (2006) The bone in the throat: some uncertain thoughts on baroque method. *International Journal of Qualitative Studies in Education* 19(6) p723-746

Morse, J (2006) The politics of evidence. *Qualitative Health Research* 16(3) p395-404

National Research Council (2002) *Scientific Research in Education* (edited by R Shavelson and L Towne). Washington, DC: National Academy Press

Preissle, J (2006) Envisioning qualitative inquiry: a view across four decades. *International Journal of Qualitative Studies in Education* 19(6) p685-696

Quigley, L (1959/1996) *The Blind Men and the Elephant.* New York: Charles Scribner's Sons

Saukko, P (2003) *Doing research in cultural studies.* CA: Sage

Schwandt, T (2006) Opposition redirected. *International Journal of Qualitative Studies in Education* 19(6) p803-810

Smith, J and Deemer, D (2000) The problem of criteria in the age of relativism. In N. Denzin and Y. Lincoln (eds) *Handbook of Qualitative Research, 3rd edition.* Thousand Oaks, Ca: Sage

Smith, J and Hodkinson, P (2005) Relativism, criteria and politics. In N. Denzin and Y. Lincoln (eds) *Handbook of Qualitative Research, 3rd edition.* Thousand Oaks, Ca: Sage

Spencer, L, Ritchie, J, Lewis, L and Dillion, L (2003) *Quality in Qualitative Evaluation: a framework for assessing research evidence.* London: Government Chief Social Researcher's Office

Stanfield, J (2006) The possible restorative justice functions of qualitative research. *International Journal of Qualitative Studies in Education* 19(6) p723-728

St. Pierre, E and Roulston, K (2006) The state of qualitative inquiry: a contested science. *International Journal of Qualitative Studies in Education,* 19(6) p673-684

Stronach, I (2006) Enlightenment and the 'Heart of Darkness': (Neo) imperialism in the Congo, and elsewhere. *International Journal of Qualitative Studies in Education* 19(6) p757-768

Stronach, I, Garratt, D, Pearce, C and Piper, H (2007) Reflexivity, the picturing of selves, the forging of method. *Qualitative Inquiry* 13(2) p179-203

Thomas, G (2004) Introduction: evidence: practice. In G Thomas and R Pring (eds) *Evidence-Based Practice in Education.* New York: Open University Press

Torrance, H (2006) Research quality and research governance in the United Kingdom. In N Denzin and M Giardina (eds) *Qualitative Inquiry and the Conservative Challenge.* Walnut Creek, Ca: Left Coast Press

2

Degrees of Denial: as global heating happens should we be educating for sustainable development or sustainable contraction?

DAVID SELBY

The Heating is happening ...

In a recent summary for policy makers, the international collectivity of scientists making up the physical science working group of the UN Intergovernmental Panel on Climate Change (IPCC) asserts that: 'Warming of the climate system is unequivocal, as is now evident from observations of increases in global average air and ocean tempera-tures, widespread melting of snow and ice, and rising global average sea level' (IPCC, 2007: 1). Confirming the anthropogenic nature of climate change and the likelihood of some 'abrupt and irreversible' impacts (*ibid*: 7), the scientists project a rise in surface air temperature of between 1.80C and 4.00C during the twenty-first century relative to the 1980-99 period and a sea level rise of between 0.18 to 0.59 metres, a rise dwarfed by any future 'rapid and dynamical' Arctic and Antarctic ice conversion events (*ibid*: 7).

Future histories, each informed by a meta-analysis of scientific papers (Lynas, 2007; Romm, 2007), offer scenarios of a twenty-first century marked by environmental disaster including drought, flooding and seasonally recurring wildfire, ongoing and massive internal and external population displacement, malnutrition and starvation, higher incidence of disease, social dislocation, violent conflict, tribalism and aggressively defensive localism, as well as the ever-lurking threat of genocide. Elizabeth Kolbert's empirically based account, Field Notes from a Catastrophe (2007), forewarns of a similarly dire future.

Scientific opinion varies as to what can be done to prevent extreme climate change. For James Lovelock, it is beyond our ken and capacity to pre-empt many of the predicted consequences. 'Our future,' he writes, 'is like that of passengers on a small pleasure boat sailing quietly above the Niagara Falls, not knowing that the engines are about to fail' (Lovelock, 2006: 6). 'The time,' says another leading climate change scientist, Konrad Steffen, 'is already five past midnight' (Kolbert, 2007: 58). Others, including IPCC (2007: 20), suggest a limited window of opportunity in which more extreme climate change scenarios can be pre-empted. 'We have a short period – very short period – in which to prevent the planet from shaking us off' (Monbiot, 2006a: 15). 'Business as usual' is not an option.

Denial and Cognitive Dissonance in Response to Global Heating

Arguably, the greatest hindrance to shaking off a 'business as usual' mindset is responses to global heating marked by an acceptance, often fulsome, of the severity of the looming crisis coupled with an ill-preparedness to follow through in terms of embracing and promoting the radical personal and societal change needed to stave off the worst effects of climate change. As such, they constitute a form of self-deceptive or furtive denial characterised by fully conscious or subliminal dissonance between perception of the problem and identified, acted upon (or not acted upon) remedies, with profoundly unhealthy ramifications for both the individual concerned and society at large. Responses of this kind are captured by Sandra Postel's prescient words of sixteen years ago:

> Psychology as much as science will determine the planet's fate ... denial, among the most paralysing of human responses ... can be as dangerous to society and the natural environment as an alcoholic's denial is to his or her own family. Because they fail to see the addiction as the principal threat to their well-being, alcoholics often end

up by destroying their own lives. Rather than facing the truth, denial's victims choose slow suicide. In a similar way, by pursuing lifestyles and economic goals that ravage the environment, we sacrifice long-term health and well-being for immediate gratification – a trade-off that cannot yield a happy ending. (Postel, 1992: 4)

To Monbiot, there is an unspoken and barely acknowledged collusion of denial between citizenry and leadership, electorate and elected:

> But the thought that worries me most is this. As people in rich countries ... begin to wake up to what science is saying, climate-change denial will look as stupid as Holocaust denial, or the insistence that AIDS can be cured with beetroot. But our response will be to demand that the government acts, while hoping that it doesn't. We will wish our governments to pretend to act. We get the moral satisfaction of saying what we know to be right, without the discomfort of doing it. My fear is that the political parties in most rich nations have already recognised this. They know that we want tough targets, but that we also want those targets to be missed. They know that we will grumble about their failure to curb climate change, but that we will not take to the streets. They know that nobody ever rioted for austerity. (Monbiot, 2006a: 41-2)

▪ For Diarmuid O'Murchu (2004), the central feature of our 'addictive trap' is 'an illusion of power and control that has become progressively compulsive, acquisitive, manipulative and destructive. ... In our addictive commitment to power, we ourselves have become quite powerless, but like all addicts we vehemently deny and disown that fact'. Joanna Macy and Molly Young Brown (1998) call the focus of addiction the 'Industrial Growth Society,' a society that cannot last in that 'it is inexorably and exponentially destroying itself' (p.23). There is ubiquitous evidence of systemic 'runaway,' they maintain, that should 'rivet our attention, summon up the blood, and bond us in collective action' but the evidence before our eyes tends to have the opposite effect making us 'want to pull down the blinds and busy ourselves with other things' (*ibid*: 26). Reminding us of the etymology of the word 'apathy', the Greek *apatheia*, literally the inability or refusal to experience pain, Macy and Young Brown identify a range of forms of Western cultural conditioning through which we repress deep concern about the planetary circumstance:

■ **Fear of pain** – Seeing pain as dysfunctional and as evidence of an inability to cope, rather than as opportunity for re-empowerment and renewal.

■ **Fear of despair** – Fearing that to admit to despair about the state of the world will undermine all we believe in and bring paralysis rather than resolve.

■ **Fear of appearing morbid** – Believing that only sanguinity and optimism are culturally appropriate indicators of and keys to success and that dystopian anguish is an indication of lack of confidence, even incompetence.

■ **Fear of guilt** – Fearing to expose the moral pain of individual and societal complicity in the abuse of peoples and other-than-human life forms around the globe and the planet itself.

■ **Fear of causing distress** – Believing it is compassionate not to distress others, especially the young, about the state of the world rather than seeing disclosure as a healthy connecting of people to the world.

■ **Fear of being unpatriotic** – Holding that to speak of things as they are will somehow harm the national fibre and interest.

■ **Fear of appearing weak and emotional** – Falling for the stoic fallacy that emotional-tinged responses are weak while impassivity is evidence of strength.

■ **Belief in the separate self** – Fearing that expressing concern about the world is simply a reflection of unprocessed inner turmoil and believing that the discrete self is the only locus of empowerment and transformation.

■ **Fear of powerlessness** – Believing that global threats are so huge and intractable that the individual can do nothing of significance. (after Macy and Young Brown [1998: 27-32]).

The consequences of such processes of repression are what Robert Gifford (2007: 209) calls 'environmental numbness' and Robert Lifton (1967) terms 'psychic numbing'. We immure ourselves from the way the world is going by divorcing our personal trajectory from the global trajectory. We immure ourselves, too, through forms of displacement or self-delusion on a spectrum from quick fix hedonism to cosy reformism. 'We live in a dark age,' concludes O'Murchu (2004: 140), 'but, alas, nobody wishes to entertain that notion. We are unable to befriend the darkness because our addictiveness and compulsiveness keep us firmly rooted in denial. The whole thing is too painful to look at, so we choose to befriend our pathology rather than befriend its deeper truth'.

Denial and Cognitive Dissonance in the Field of Education for Sustainable Development

A befriending of our pathology afflicts those positioned along the reform to transformation continuum in their responses to global heating, including many proponents of education for sustainable development.

The Learning and Skills Council, a body responsible for the UK further education sector, argues in its *Strategy for Sustainable Development* (2005: 3) that 'we are living in an unsustainable world' not least because 'global temperatures are rising faster than previously recorded'. Alongside this, it identifies 'the maintenance of high and stable levels of economic growth and employment' as a key sustainable development objective and, in language that resonates with globalisation-speak, it continues:

> Experience shows there is a strong business case for sustainable development. Businesses, companies, colleges and learning providers that adopt environmental management systems can make significant financial savings. They can also enhance their reputation, gain access to new markets and better motivate their staff. (p.4)

The conception of the humanity-nature relationship within the document is one of nature as a resource to be managed, having instrumental rather than intrinsic value.

The same is the case in the pronouncements of Forum for the Future, the influential UK sustainable development charity with a significant educational arm to its work. Noting in the presumptuously titled report on its 2003 activities, *Sustainable Development – the only game in town*, that 'evidence of unsustainable development kept piling up' (Forum for the Future, 2004: 1), Forum rehearses its 'Five Capitals' framework for responding to the global environmental crisis in which nature, human beings and human communities and forms of social organisation are viewed as capital assets alongside financial and manufactured capital (*ibid*: 3, 5, 8, 9, 12). Nature is conceived of as resource – 'the stock or flow of energy and material' (p.3) – underpinning a system of capitalistic development that needs to be husbanded properly to safeguard its upward trajectory. The response to the global crisis is better care of assets for *status quo* maintenance. Following from this, Forum's emphasis on skills-based 'sustainability literacy' in its Higher Education Partnership for Sustainability with 18 UK universities comes as no surprise:

> A sustainability literate person will be equipped with a number of intellectual and practical tools that enable them to make decisions and act in a way that is likely to contribute positively to sustainable development. They will be able to make decisions on specific matters, such as advising on financial investment, buying food or writing new policy for prisons, by applying the 'at the same time' rule – that is, taking environmental, social and economic considerations into account simultaneously, not separately. (Parkin *et al*, 2004: 9)

While recommending action, the prescription for educational change is apathetic, in the sense used earlier of inability or refusal to confront and experience pain. The concept of 'sustainability literacy,' much vaunted across the field of education for sustainable development (see, for instance, DfES, 2003; John Foster Associates, 2006) is itself objectivist in its explicit or implicit emotion avoidance – even in skills terms, the skills and capacities for handling despair, distress, pain, guilt and grief are not addressed – and in its failure to position the transformative dispositions and capabilities of the individual within a conscious reconnecting with the flow of life.

This phenomenon is not restricted to the United Kingdom. In their report to Macquarie University and the Australian Department of the Environment and Heritage, *Change in Curricula and Graduate Skills Towards Sustainability*, Daniella Tilbury and colleagues (2004: 3) write: 'Education for Sustainability involves students and educators in a process of active learning and futures thinking, and addresses the generic skill needs of business and industry'. The skills list offered recites critical, creative and future-thinking skills, needs assessment and action-oriented skills, interpersonal and intercultural skills, the skills of dealing with uncertainty, and problem solving skills (*ibid*).

Important as they are, they are set within a frame of the 'generic skills needs of business and industry', eschewing alternative frames and dispositions crucial to a context of looming or actual threat to civilisation. The emphasis on skills, as with the Learning and Skills Council and Forum for the Future, also tends to obfuscate the centrality of a values response to a threatened world. None of the education for sustainable development proposals reviewed here calls for the curricular treatment of themes and issues that might reasonably be seen as imperative for actively addressing the deepening multiple crisis syndrome of global heating. This point will be returned to later.

A fundamental issue for proponents of education for sustainable development is the relevance of continuing to talk about development. As James Lovelock (2006) so powerfully puts it:

> (W)hen change was slow or non-existent, we might have had time to establish sustainable development, or even have continued for a while with business as usual, but now is much too late; the damage has already been done. To expect sustainable development or a trust in business as usual to be viable policies is like expecting a lung cancer victim to be cured by stopping smoking; both measures deny the existence of the Earth's disease, the fever brought on by a plague of people. (p3)

For Lovelock, 'what we need is a sustainable retreat' (*ibid*: 7). He adds: 'We need people of the world to sense the real and present danger so that they will spontaneously mobilise and unstintingly bring about an orderly and sustainable withdrawal to a world where we try to live in harmony with Gaia' (*ibid*: 150).

Preferring the softer and more ecological concept of 'contraction', a concept devoid of militaristic connotations and suggesting the systemic rather than the systematic, the organic rather than the lockstep, let me examine what 'education for sustainable contraction' in the face of radical climate change might look like.

Education for Sustainable Contraction (ESC): Nailing Ten Propositions to the Door of the Academy

On 31 October 1517 Martin Luther nailed ninety-five propositions to the door of the Castle Church in Wittenberg, Germany. The propositions attacked the widespread practice of the Catholic Church of selling indulgences, paper certificates guaranteeing relief from punishment in Purgatory, to those who had committed sins. This is regarded as the seminal moment in the Reformation of the Western Christian Church (Davies: 1996: 484-5). It has not gone unnoticed by climate change commentators that the hypocrisy and cognitive dissonance of the pre-Reformation period finds its echo in the thinking and practices of those accepting, but not following through on the consequences of accepting, the climate change threat. A notable example is carbon offsetting. 'Just as in the fifteenth and sixteenth centuries you could sleep with your sister, kill and lie without eternal damnation', suggests Monbiot (2006a: 210), 'today you can leave your windows open while the heating is on, drive and fly without endangering the climate, as long as you give your ducats to one of the companies selling indulgences'. Inspired by this connection (see also Monbiot, 2006b), ten propositions for Education for Sustainable Contraction are offered below.

Before exploring each of these propositions, it is important to identify what frequently recurring features of education for sustainable development would be markedly absent from, or significantly less ubiquitous within, an ESC landscape:

- The uncritical or tacit acceptance of unrestrained economic growth and continued globalisation, fed by rampant consumerism

- An instrumentalist and utilitarian view of nature, emphasising the 'desirability of sustaining those natural systems that are conducive to *human* flourishing' (Bonnett, 1999: 315), with its correlative denial of the intrinsic value of the natural world and of human embeddedness in nature

- A managerialist orientation to sustainability in which 'natural resources' and the world are looked upon as what Bonnett (*ibid*: 317), citing Mitchum (1997), calls 'a spaceship in need of an operating manual'

- Absorption with technical fixes for unsustainability, with skills development of the learner prioritised and values issues left on the rhetorical shelf

- A conception of change potential as fundamentally individual as against individuated, ie the person acting from a sense of being largely alone even if working in tandem with others, rather than from a sense of their orchestrated and holographic enfoldment within the social and environmental whole (O'Murchu, 91-3)

- An exteriority of focus (issues in the world out there) as against a dynamic interplay between interiority and exteriority in processes of personal and social transformation

Uprooting these harmful features would clear the ground for Education for Sustainable Contraction (ESC):

ESC: Proposition 1: A concerted effort is needed in the light of the threat of radical climate change to confront denial by moving learner assumptions, understandings and responses towards disequilibrium (fomenting dissipative structures).

ESC: Proposition 2: Given the likely impending severity of global heating, Education for Sustainable Contraction needs to address despair, pain, grief and loss.

Global heating is beginning to turn the world on its business-as-usual head, exposing the fragility of the normal and the vulnerability of the taken-for-granted. As Monbiot (2005: 23) puts it:

> Everything we thought was good turns out to be bad. It is an act of kindness to travel to your cousin's wedding. Now it is also an act of cruelty. It is a good thing to light the streets at night. Climate change tells us it kills more people than it saves. ... Climate change demands a reversal of our moral compass, for which we are plainly unprepared.

Classrooms at various levels are marked by the steady return to a minimal swing of the pendulum agitated by the learning dynamic, so as to resume a more or less settled condition. 'What', asks Ilya Prigogine (1989: 396), 'if we turn the pendulum on its head?' It is difficult to predict what will happen. The notion of the upturned pendulum, Prigogine argues, has been 'ideologically suppressed' in that its message is inconvenient for a culture that seeks to dominate and suppress nature (*ibid*: 396-7). For confronting a world that threatens to make castles built of sand of our assumptions, the notion acquires huge consequence, as does Prigogine's concept of 'dissipative structures' within self-organising systems. Prigogine distinguishes between systems at equilibrium or near-equilibrium where huge disturbances would be required to effect radical change, and hence where creativity is low, and far-from-equilibrium systems. In the case of the latter, a fluctuation can induce movement to disequilibrium – dissipation – at which point the system responds by bringing to bear on a situation as wide and coherent a range of forces as is necessary to effect a new level of (complexified) equilibrium. It is at far-from-equilibrium where the potential for deep creativity lies (Capra, 1996: 180-3) and, within learning community dynamics, where reversals of the moral compass, held back by denial, are more likely to happen.

Confronting despair, pain, grief and loss within the community of learners is a likely harbinger of dissipative structures. At a recent conference on Sustainability and the Curriculum, I found myself in a small minority arguing for 'gloom and doom' as vital for transformative learning. Most of those present regarded 'gloom and doom' as disempowering for the learner. For me, their position smacked of denial, and also of reluctance to recognise that, for an ecological or holistic worldview, life and death are marked by dynamical unity, 'the cycle of birth-death-rebirth' (O'Murchu, 2004: 190).

From within a quantum theological frame, O'Murchu writes of the importance of the 'Calvary moment' (*ibid*), encapsulating the idea that transformation entails a conscious and thoroughgoing progression by groups and individuals through despair towards empowerment, healing and renewal. The 'Great Turning,' as Joanna Macy calls it, involves breaking through denial to confront the pain of the world, heroic holding actions to stop things getting worse, analysis of the structural causes of the damage wreaked by the Great Industrial Society allied to the nurturing of alternative institutions and, most fundamentally, a cognitive, spiritual and perceptual re-awakening to the wholeness of everything (Macy and Young Brown, 1998: 17-22). Macy's work on despair and empowerment provides a powerful canon of activities and exercises for breaking out of denial to connect with the state of the world (Macy, 1983, Macy, 1991; Macy and Young Brown, 1998). Such exercises would be the food and drink of education for sustainable contraction.

ESC: Proposition 3: The view of human<>nature relationship needs to shift from the doministic, instrumental and exploitative to embeddedness and intrinsic valuing, from a shallow ecological to a deep ecological paradigm.

ESC: Proposition 4: The poetic dimension of sustainability needs serious cultivation.

As has been noted, common to articulations of education for sustainable development is representation of nature as resource. This is indicative of collusion with the dominant corporate paradigm but also suggests that the precocious and headstrong infant that was ESD in the 1990s paid insufficient heed to a heritage of eco-philosophical responses to the question of humanity's relationship to the environment, each response offering its own insights on how to live ethically and responsively on the planet. Had the infant listened, in particular, to deep ecology, ESD might have thought more deeply about the human<>nature relationship and divested itself of some of its anthropocentrism, at least giving space in its debates to the biospherical egalitarian position (Selby, 2006: 359). Key principles of deep ecology include:

- The well-being and flourishing of both human and other-than-human life have value in themselves

- Richness and diversity of life forms (and cultures) are valuable in themselves

- Human interference with the other-than-human world is excessive

- Quality of life matters more than standard of living (after Devall and Sessions, 1998: 147)

Re-bonding with nature would be a key goal of ESC and would involve the cultivation of the poetic dimension of human awareness, thus marrying sense with sensibility (Selby, 2006: 361). Michael Bonnett (1999: 321) writes

> At the heart of the matter is the question of the adequacy of rationality to resolve issues in an area as complex, subtle and multi-dimensional ... as environmental concern, not least from the motives and values embedded in modern rationality itself. ... The central point here is that rationality itself is not neutral; it expresses certain aspirations towards the world, notably to classify, explain, predict, evaluate and, as far as modern rationality is concerned,

increasingly to exploit it. Arguably, it is the growing ascendancy of such motives and our increasing power to implement them that has led to our current environmental predicament.

The cultivation of the poetic would end the marginalisation that emotional and eco-spiritual ways of knowing – attunement, awe, celebration, enchantment, intuition, reverence, wonder, and oceanic feelings of connectedness – have experienced under education for sustainable development. ESC would, therefore, embrace a much more multi-dimensional epistemology in which the learner would be nurtured to feel both the beauty and pain of the Earth through the intimate and innocent eye:

> To see a World in a Grain of Sand
> And a Heaven in a Wild Flower
> Hold Infinity in the palm of your hand
> And Eternity in an hour.

> William Blake, *Auguries of Innocence* (Hayward, 1968:243)

ESC: Proposition 5: Marginalised educations within education for sustainable development will be of pivotal importance.

ESC Proposition 6: With global heating under way, sustainability education and emergency education need to fold together.

It is perhaps indicative of the 'business as usual' mindset pervading the field of education for sustainable development that, while holistic and integrative in original intention (UNCED, 1992) and, at the level of rhetoric, still so characterised (see, for instance, UNESCO, 2002: 8, 10), the insights of certain key social, political and moral educations are virtually ignored.

Confronted with all the societal ramifications of potential, some would say inevitable, degree-by-degree global heating, giving peace education a central place within the panoply of sustainability educations would seem essential. A field concerned with non-violence, conflict avoidance and conflict resolution, confronting and unpacking negative and enemy images of the 'other', and processes and outcomes of direct and structural violence (Smith and Carson, 1998) would have the potential to bring wisdom and insight to learners facing the looming prospect or immediacy of what is being predicted. For similar reasons, anti-discriminatory education, concerned with confronting all the negative and hegemonic centrisms that foment societal and inter-human injustice, and with dissecting inner and outwardly-manifesting processes of othering (Plumwood, 1993, 1996; Selby, 2001), needs to be brought to an ESC agenda. In helping learners confront ubiquitous social, political and media global heating denial, the 'crap detecting' skills (to borrow the incisive term of Postman and Weingartner [1969]) and insights of media literacy education would also be given prominence (Duncan *et al*, 2000).

The gulf that has so far characterised the relationship between education for sustainable development and emergency education will urgently need to be bridged as the heating happens. Emergency education, that is, education in crisis or disaster contexts occasioned by armed strife and/or environmental cataclysm, has achieved increasing prominence since the end of the Cold War period (Kagawa, 2005; Kagawa and Selby 2006). Fumiyo Kagawa (forthcoming) explains that, as the world moves ever more inexorably into multiple crisis syndrome, the theory and practice of sustainability and emergency need to coalesce. The future histories touched upon earlier make clear that emergency education is soon not going to be something to be applied 'out there'. Everybody and everywhere will be in emergency.

It follows that educational providers in different localities and regions will need to provide concrete life skills learning in anticipation, or from direct experience, of the kinds of environmental disaster likely to strike locally. An indication of what will be required can be drawn from the Armenian national life skills curriculum in which, given the frequency and extremity of earthquakes in the region, earthquake preparedness and response skills figure in each grade of a grade 1-10 life skills programme (Soukhudyan, 2000).

ESC: Proposition 7: Formal and informal education programmes need to offer alternative and localised conceptions of the good life and good citizen (or good denizen).

ESC: Proposition 8: Cosy assumptions about the relationship between education for sustainability and education for citizenship need unpacking.

In *Earth Democracy: Justice, Sustainability and Peace* (2005), Vandana Shiva makes a powerful case for localism of response to the global crisis of unsustainability. 'Conservation of the earth's resources and creation of sustainable livelihoods,' she writes (p.xvi,10), 'are most caringly, creatively, efficiently and equitably achieved at the local level. Localisation of economies is a social and ecological imperative'. For Shiva, localism allows for 'living democracy' integrated with a 'sustenance economy' within which 'people can influence the decisions over the food we eat, the water we drink, and the health care and education we have' (*ibid*).

There has been an all-too-cosy connection between education for sustainable development, on the one hand, and citizenship education (including what is called 'global citizenship education') and education for democracy, on the other. The respective educations are, more often than not, assumed to enjoy a dovetailed relationship (see, for instance, Bourne, 2005; National Assembly of Wales, 2005; QCAA, Wales, 2002). A thorny, but largely untouched, problem concerns how representative democracy drawing upon an electorate immured in and, on that account, not readily teased from, a pervasive consumerist ethic can be squared with an environmental narrative predicated on the finiteness of the Earth. If we embrace the notion of finiteness and the ecological imperatives deriving from it, 'certain policies are proscribed', writes Bonnett (1999: 315). He elaborates:

> They are in effect not only removed from the area of democratic debate, but set the parameters within which democratic debate can be allowed to function. ... Insofar as such enframing is broad in scope, it is tantamount to defining a conception of the good life to which citizens need to be brought to conform and thus both runs counter to the assumption of democracy of valuing diversity of view and holds the danger of peripheralising democracy as a contingent value, instrumental to achieving the public acceptance of these imperatives.

Shiva's 'living democracy' provides a means of negotiating the seeming impasse. It is almost certainly the case that citizenship education focused upon representative democracy will never sit easily with the sustained and draconian intervention of government, regarded as essential by some such as Romm (2007). For Shiva, 'it is essential to dispel the notion that globalisation is natural and inevitable' (2005: 106) and that we see it as a political and profiteering process that continues to encroach on the commons, ie that held to be common property or of shared accessibility, through appropriation, privatisation, exclusion and 'the enclosure of minds and imagination' whereby the global market is portrayed by its adherents as the only way forward (ibid: 20).

The alternative path Shiva advocates is the actual lived experience of two-thirds of humankind, in 'which humans produce in balance with nature and reproduce society through partnerships, mutuality, and reciprocity' (ibid: 17). Turning globalisation on its head, Shiva envisages a future in which the 'most intense relationships are at the local level and the thinnest interactions at the international level' with decisions being taken 'at the level closest to where the impact is felt' (ibid: 64).

Localisation would not only offer a more fertile arena for participatory democracy to flourish but, based on a keener, immediately lived, appreciation of the 'interdependence between nature and culture, humans and other species' (ibid: 82), would open the way for a more biocentric and less consumerist and exploitative democracy. Following the principle of subsidiarity, the centralised draconian approach to preventing perilous levels of global heating would stand in negative correlation with 'living democracy', that is, like a thermostat, only being triggered if the climate change determinations of localities fell short.

In educational terms, subsidiarity would also apply to curriculum, with thinnest input into curriculum framing emanating from the national level. Learning would involve a rebalancing of the mind/hand interface through local craft learning and craft apprenticeships. Generally within localised living democracies and sustenance economies, there would be a move away from learning as expert induction to a livelihood, communitarian orientation fostering new 'tools of conviviality' (Illich, 1973).

Within such a scenario, the weighting within citizenship education would shift towards local participatory democracy with commensurately reduced emphasis on national citizenship. In treating the global level, education would be responsive to the need to globalise 'compassion, not greed' (Shiva, 2005: 115). The notion of citizenship might give way to that of denizenship, a denizen being an inhabitant or occupant of a particular place, the term connoting primacy of immediate context while also neatly sidestepping the built-in anthropocentrism of citizenship in that a denizen can be either human or other-than-human.

ESC: Proposition 9: A more radical tilt away from mechanistic thinking to holistic ways of mediating and interpreting reality is urgently called for, with keener appreciation given in learning to the complex, multiple ramifications and reverberations of actions.

ESC: Proposition 10: Everyone has to understand and come to terms with the fact that we are threatening our own existence. To confront this requires a Copernican revolution in aims, structures, processes of education and, perhaps, in the loci of learning.

While some sustainability educators have emphasised that social transformation towards sustainability calls for a relinquishing of the pervasive mechanistic way of seeing the world and a radical shift to holistic and systemic perception (Selby, 2006; Sterling, 2007), the field of education for sustainable development remains habituated to mechanism (Selby, 2007), an argument that has been implicitly and explicitly present throughout this chapter. It will not be further elaborated here. As the heating happens, education cannot afford the self-indulgence of being other than holistic and systemic.

If habituation to mechanism and a 'business as usual' mindset afflict those embracing change, how much more so is this the case within schools and universities. Mechanism, writes Richardson (1990: 54), is 'institutionalised in all sorts of structures and career patterns'. It is certain that, as the heating happens, education and educational institutions as we presently know them will be deeply disrupted and, if unresponsive to the need for transformation, will disintegrate as people find other, more relevant, loci for learning what they have to learn.

I leave the last word to George Monbiot:

> For the campaign against climate change is an odd one. Unlike almost all other public protests which have preceded it, it is a campaign not for abundance but for austerity. It is a campaign not for more freedom but for less. Strangest of all, it is a campaign not just against other people, but also against ourselves. (2006a: 215)

David Selby

References

Bonnett, M (1999) Education for sustainable development: A coherent philosophy for environmental education? *Cambridge Journal of Education* 29(3) p313-324

Bourne, D (2005) Interconnectedness versus interdependence: reflections in response to David Selby. Zeitschrift fuer internationale Bildungsforschung und Entwicklungspaedagogic (*Journal for International Educational Research and Development Education*) 28(1) p29-34

Capra, F (1996) *The Web of Life: a new scientific understanding of living systems.* New York: Anchor/Doubleday

Davies, N (1996) *Europe: a history.* Oxford: Oxford University Press

Department for Education and Skills (DfES) (2003) *Sustainable Development Action Plan for Education and Skills.* London: DfES

Devall, B and Sessions, G (1998) Deep ecology. In L Pojman (ed) *Environmental Ethics: readings in theory and application.* Belmont CA: Wadsworth

Duncan, B, Pungente, J and Shepherd, R (2000) Media education in Canada. In T Goldstein and D Selby (eds) *Weaving Connections: educating for peace, social and environmental Justice.* Toronto: Sumach

Forum for the Future (2004) *Sustainable Development – the only game in town: Annual report 2004.* London: Forum for the Future

Gifford, R (2007) Environmental psychology and sustainable development: expansion, maturation and challenge. *Journal of Social Issues* 63(1) p199-212

Hayward, J (1968) *The Penguin Book of English Verse.* London: Penguin

Illich, I (1973) *Tools for Conviviality.* New York: Harper and Row

IPCC (2007) *Summary for Policymakers of the Synthesis Report of the IPCC Fourth Assessment Report.* Geneva: IPCC Secretariat

John Foster Associates (2006) *Sustainability Literacy: embedding sustainability into the curriculum of Scotland's universities and colleges.* Edinburgh: Scottish Further and Higher Education Council

Kagawa, F (2005) Emergency education: a critical review of the field. *Comparative Education* 41(4) p487-503

Kagawa, F (forthcoming) Whose emergencies and who decides? Insights from emergency education for a more anticipatory education for sustainable development, *International Journal of Innovation and Sustainable Development*

Kagawa, F and Selby, D (2006) 'Now she is singing!' Emergency education in theory and practice. *Escalate newsletter* (newsletter of the Higher Education Academy Subject Centre for Education) 6(August) p13-14

Kolbert, E (2007) *Field Notes from a Catastrophe: a frontline report on climate change.* London: Bloomsbury

Learning and Skills Council (2005) *From Here to Sustainability: the Learning and Skills Council's strategy for sustainable development.* Coventry: LSC

Lifton, R (1967) *Death in Life: survivors of Hiroshima.* New York: Random House

Lovelock, J (2006) *The Revenge of Gaia: why the Earth is fighting back – and how we can still save humanity.* London: Allen Lane

Lynas, M (2007) *Six Degrees: our future on a hotter planet.* London: Fourth Estate

Macy, J (1983) *Despair and Personal Power in the Nuclear Age.* Philadelphia, Pa: New Society

Macy, J (1991) *World as Lover, World as Self.* Berkeley, Ca: Parallax

Macy, J and M Young Brown (1998) *Coming Back to Life: Practices to reconnect our lives, our world.* Gabriola Island, BC: New Society

Mitchum, C (1997) The sustainability question. In R Gottleib (ed) *The Ecological Community*. London: Routledge

Monbiot, G (2005) A restraint of liberty. *The Guardian*, 24th May, p23

Monbiot, G (2006a) *Heat: how to stop the planet from burning*. Toronto: Doubleday Canada

Monbiot, G (2006b) Selling indulgences. http://www.monbiot.com/archives/2006/10/19/selling-indulgences/ (accessed August 2007).

National Assembly of Wales (2005) *Global Citizenship Secondary School Map – education for sustainable development and global citizenship, Circular no. 11/2005*. Cardiff: National Assembly of Wales

O'Murchu, D (2004) *Quantum Theology: spiritual implications of the new physics*. New York: Crossroad

Parkin, S, Johnson, A, Buckland, H, Brookes, F and White, E (2004) *Learning and Skills for Sustainable Development: developing a sustainability literate society*. London: Forum for the Future/Higher Education Partnership for Sustainability

Plumwood, V (1996) Androcentrism and anthropocentrism: Parallels and politics. *Ethics and the Environment* 1(2) p119-132

Plumwood, V (1993) *Feminism and the Mastery of Nature*. New York: Routledge

Postel, S (1992) Denial in the decisive decade. In L Brown and L. Starke (eds) *State of the World 1992: a Worldwatch Institute report on progress towards a sustainable society*. New York: W.W.Norton

Postman, N and Weingartner, C (1969) *Teaching as a Subversive Activity*. New York: Delacorte

Prigogine, I (1989) The philosophy of instability. *Futures* 21(4) p396-400

Qualifications, Curriculum and Assessment Authority for Wales (2002) *Education for Sustainable Development and Global Citizenship*. Cardiff: QCAA, Wales

Richardson, R (1990) *Daring to be a Teacher*. Stoke-on-Trent: Trentham

Romm, J (2007) *Hell and High Water: global warming – the solution and the politics - and what we should do*. New York: William Morrow

Selby, D (2001) The signature of the whole: radical interconnectedness and its implications for global and environmental education. *Encounter: Education for Meaning and Social Justice* 14(1) p5-16

Selby, D (2006) The firm and shaky ground of education for sustainable development. *Journal of Geography in Higher Education* 30(2) p351-365

Selby, D (2007) Reaching into the holomovement: a Bohmian perspective on social learning for sustainability. In A Wals (ed) *Social Learning towards a Sustainable World: principles, perspectives, and praxis*. Wageningen: Wageningen Academic

Shiva, V (2005) *Earth Democracy: justice, sustainability and peace*. London: Zed

Smith, D and Carson, T (1998) *Educating for a Peaceful Future*. Toronto: Kagan and Woo

Soukhudyan, M (2000) Life skills in Armenia. Paper presented at the Future of Our Children Education for Peace International Meeting, University of Geneva, 4-8 September 2000

Sterling, S (2007) Riding the Storm: towards a connective cultural consciousness. In A Wals (ed) *Social Learning towards a Sustainable World: principles, perspectives, and praxis*. Wageningen: Wageningen Academic

Tilbury,D, Podger, D, and Reid, A (2004) *Change in Curricula and Graduate Skills towards Sustainability: final report*. Australian Government Department of the Environment and Heritage/Macquarie University

United Nations Conference on Environment and Development (UNCED) (1992) *Agenda 21/Rio Declaration on Environment and Development*. New York: United Nations Department of Public Information

UNESCO (2002) *Education for Sustainability: from Rio to Johannesburg: lessons learnt from a decade of commitment*. Paris: UNESCO

3

Vulnerability – Analytical Concept or Rhetorical Idiom?

FRANK FUREDI

Introduction

This chapter explores the way that the rhetoric of vulnerability contributes to the diagnosis of contemporary social problems in the UK and the US. It draws attention to the conceptual inflation of vulnerability in public discourse and the social sciences, and argues that the appeal of this idiom reflects changing views on the constitution of personhood. Vulnerability has emerged as a widely used concept that purports to signify an important dimension of the human condition. Many believe that it is an important and valuable concept for capturing the experience of individuals and communities. Yet, 'the concept of vulnerability is an extraordinarily elastic concept, capable of being stretched to cover almost any person, group, or situation, and then of being snapped back to describe a narrow range of characteristics like age or incarceration' (Levine, 2004: 398). Despite or because of its conceptual incoherence, vulnerability has also become a powerful metaphor used in everyday vernacular. Consequently, this chapter considers the rhetorical strategies deployed in the construction of 'the vulnerable' so as to account for its use by competing claim-makers in public life. Such understanding is necessary for all those interested in confronting the language of power.

The discovery of vulnerability

Some terms express the prevailing emotional and cultural mood in a way that does not require explanation or definition. Terms like trauma, stress and self-esteem have become taken-for-granted concepts through which people gain meaning for the problems of life (Furedi: 2004). They express a therapeutic sensibility that pervades popular culture, the world of politics, the workplace, schools and universities etc. The therapeutic culture provides a script through which emotional deficits 'make their way into the cultural vernacular' and become available for 'the construction of everyday reality' (Gergen, 1990: 362). One of the clearest manifestations of this trend is the widespread and unquestioned use of the term 'vulnerable' to signify important dimensions of everyday reality. Vulnerability and its companion terms such as vulnerable groups are used to represent and characterise a growing variety of groups and people. The terms vulnerable man and vulnerable women hint at unspecified deficits but can connote the positive attribute of someone in touch with their feelings: 'Hey we love a vulnerable man' observes a report on blind dating (*Coventry Evening News*: 2005).

In the media, vulnerability has emerged as one of the dominant frames through which social problems are communicated to the public. It works as a form of rhetorical idiom that successfully draws on the vernacular resources of society. Rhetorical idioms are defined as 'definitional complexes, utilising language that situates condition-categories in moral universes [that] draw upon a cluster of images' that resonate with the public imagination (Ibarra and Kitsuse 2003: 25-26). Ibarra and Kitsuse point to examples such as the 'rhetoric of loss' which evokes nostalgic sensibilities or the 'rhetoric of unreason' that provokes images of 'manipulation of controversy' amongst an audience of the lay public. In a similar way, what we characterise as the rhetoric of vulnerability works as a rhetorical idiom that situates particular individuals and groups and their experience within a context of powerlessness and lack of agency.

An analysis of UK and US based newspapers through the database LexisNexis and the index of *The Times* and *New York Times* indicates that since the 1990s, groups that are presumed to deserve economic, social or moral support are frequently described as 'vulnerable'. Government reports on health, education, crime and welfare continually refer to the targets of their policy as 'vulnerable children', 'vulnerable adults' or just as 'the vulnerable'. Such official reports echo the media narrative of vulnerability which is characteristically imprecise about the meaning of this term. The past three decades have seen a steady expansion of people and groups who are defined or who present themselves as vulnerable. In the 1960s and 1970s the term was mainly but very selectively applied to children and the elderly. In the 1980s, ethnic minorities, the homeless, single parents, the mentally ill, people in care and the unemployed were added to this list.

UK newspapers indicate that since the 1990s vulnerability has encompassed the experience of a new range of emotional distress: 'depressed men', 'stressed employees' and 'career women'. In more recent times, young Muslim men, university students, teenagers under pressure to be thin, people addicted to Internet pornography are only a small sample of the ever growing constituencies who have been characterised as vulnerable (*The Observer*, 2003). 'One law for the rich, one for the vulnerable' ran the headline of one broadsheet (*The Independent*: 2003). A similar pattern is evident in the US. By the 1990s the term vulnerable was commonly used to refer to virtually every group facing a difficult predicament. One *New York Times* (1998) headline: 'We're All Vulnerable Now', illustrates this sensibility.

Yet it is worth noting that prior to the mid 1980s the term vulnerability was used selectively, in relation to a discrete set of circumstances, and rarely referred to an entire social group. Occasionally it was used in relation to children and the elderly, when confronted with a specific predicament. The earliest reference to a vulnerable group in *LexisNexis* was in June 1969 in connexion with the appointment of a Presidential Consultant charged with organising a Conference on Food and Nutrition by the Nixon White House. Nixon stated that this conference would seek to develop new survey methods to keep track of malnutrition levels and improve the nutrition of the nation's 'most vulnerable groups' (*New York Times*, 12 June, 1969).

Until the 1980s those depicted as members of a vulnerable group were seen to suffer from a specific impediment: the elderly because they were isolated from the members of their community. In one article those who were housebound were vulnerable because they ate less food than other elderly people. Single mothers were portrayed as vulnerable because of the predicament they faced due to a shortage of housing. Ethnic minorities were depicted as vulnerable due to the discrimination they faced from others (*The Times*, 1968; 1973; 1974).

In contemporary times it is no longer necessary to specify in what way a group is vulnerable. The symbolic currency of vulnerability is so powerful that its meaning is taken for granted. No longer are people vulnerable to just one or two problems. Today the elderly, the disabled or children are frequently represented as groups whose very existence is defined by their vulnerability and for such groups the condition of vulnerability constitutes a presupposition of their existence.

Since the early 1990s, vulnerable is increasingly used as an intrinsic quality of an individual or group rather than referring to an episode in their life. Thus a *New York Times* (2005) article about disaster victims was headlined: 'The Vulnerable Become More Vulnerable'. In certain circumstances it is no longer even necessary to mention any specific group since we can take for granted that we know who we are talking about. The statement 'this innovative project will address the specific health needs of a wide variety of vulnerable groups' speaks for itself, as does the claim that there are 'vulnerable groups of people at both ends of the age spectrum' (*Aberdeen Press* and *Journal*, 2001; *The Guardian*, 1998). These are people who clearly cannot manage on their own.

The identity of vulnerability is both bestowed and embraced. The tendency to represent vulnerability as an important dimension of one's identity has been appropriated by advocacy organisations and pressure groups to legitimate their cause. One goal of the campaigning group 'Fathers for Justice' is to gain *recognition* for lone fathers as a vulnerable group which therefore deserves support. Similarly the 'campaign group Fathers Direct warned that single dads were one of the most vulnerable groups in the country' (*The Express*, 2000). A spokesperson for the Countryside Alliance declared that 'we have become a vulnerable minority' (*The Daily Telegraph*, 2005b).

This demand for public support on the ground that a group is powerless or the underdog is advanced by an International Labour Union report warning about 'fear in the workplace'. Guy Standing, one of the authors of the report, stated that 'unless this is reversed, the vulnerable will become more vulnerable' (*The Guardian*, 2004). Two advocates of workers' rights agree: 'We believe sympathy action in support of weak and vulnerable workers is just as relevant today as it was when the Trade Disputes Act 1906 first protected such action' (*The Guardian*, 2005b). That trade unions frame their claim for workers' rights through embracing the identity of vulnerability is influenced by the presumption that this rhetorical idiom resonates with a wider cultural imagination.

A warrant for claims-making

Claims-making involves making statements about problems that deserve or ought to deserve the attention of society. A claim constitutes a warrant for recognition or some form of entitlement. Today many claims for support draw on taken-for-granted assumptions about vulnerability. Joel Best (1999) describes how a new social problem depends on how the public, the press, and policy makers are used to talking about already familiar problems. Since vulnerability signifies a negative or problematic condition over which the individual or group has little control, it possesses considerable rhetorical appeal for public support. The vulnerable are victims who are 'innocent' and hence 'moral' as Loseke notes (2003, 123). The rhetoric of vulnerability legitimates claims for moral recognition, and thus offers distinct benefits.

Social problems are invariably represented as a harmful condition where the 'condition-category is inhabited by a *victim* [and the] causal agent of harm': the victimiser (Loseke, 2003: 121). Such causal agents, even impersonal ones, can be personified as the symbol of everything that's wrong. For example, the problems 'caused' by capitalism can be attributed to the acts of the 'greedy' capitalist. The rhetoric of vulnerability constructs actual and potential victims, without constructing a distinct group of victimisers. The vulnerable suffer from harm for which it is difficult to assign direct responsibility. Consequently support for the vulnerable need not offend any distinct constituency. In principal it is a cause to which all sections of society can give support. That is why, by the mid 1990s, 'vulnerable' had become a catch-all political expression, used by both the left and right to lend authority for their arguments. The word 'vulnerable' has been used to describe beggars themselves and also the public who must suffer their existence. For example, after John Major launched an attack on beggars he was fiercely criticised for his 'small-minded attack on the most vulnerable' (*The Independent*, 1994). Similarly a year later Jack Straw was also criticised as uncompassionate by the left wing press for his attacks on beggars. He responded by framing his case as an attempt to stand up for the vulnerable public (*The Guardian*, 1995).

Competing appeals to the authority of the vulnerable indicates that the term has achieved the status of what political sociologists characterise as a *master frame* or a broad interpretative perspective on social ills that resonate with ideals that prevail in popular culture. Today equality or safety often serve as master frames for the promotion of campaigns and causes. Such frames are often transmitted through a diffuse and flexible rhetoric able to resonate with groups that hold contradictory political positions (Williams and Williams, 1995: 194). As the debate on begging indicates, the master frame of vulnerability enjoys widespread consensus and can be adopted by otherwise competing groups and parties.

Competition for the status of the most vulnerable is evident in the UK press. For example, 'the vulnerable' can be used to refer to either the 'unborn child' or young pregnant women. In 1997 a *Daily Mail* article, which equated abortion and child abuse, ran with the headline: 'We must care again for the vulnerable' (*Daily Mail*, 1997). In 2005, the Archbishop of Westminster argued against abortion, claiming that 'the world's most vulnerable lives hang in the balance' (*The Daily Telegraph*, 2005a). In contrast, articles which express a prochoice orientation describe pregnant women as 'vulnerable'. In 2002, *The Independent* criticised the then Conservative Party Deputy Leader Michael Ancram for opposing the sale of the abortion pill: 'So much for the Conservative Party's concern for the vulnerable'.

With so much moral authority attached to the status of the vulnerable, it is not surprising that it has acquired positive connotations. By the late nineties and the early 21st century people were positively encouraged to acknowledge their vulnerability. 'Parents told to nurture a generation of boys who know it's ok to be vulnerable' is the title of a feature in *The Independent* (2000). The positive connotation of being vulnerable is frequently transmitted: 'As a vulnerable human being, Rowan Williams lacks deviousness and conspiratorial skills' was the verdict of *The Times* (2002) on the newly appointed Archbishop of Canterbury. Similarly a profile of the Hollywood legend Humphrey Bogart alludes to the 'vulnerable man behind the tough-guy myth', noting he was a 'great romantic' (*The Sunday Telegraph*, 2004).

The model of vulnerability

The ascendancy of the term vulnerability as a distinctive cultural metaphor is paralleled by its growing usage in the social sciences. What is remarkable is that the growth and expansive remit of this rhetorical idiom follows a pattern that is strikingly similar to its trajectory in everyday culture. The database of the *International Bibliography of the Social Sciences* between 1951 and 2005 contains 588 academic journal articles that contain the term vulnerability in its title. Of these, six were published in the 1950s, six in the 1960s, fourteen in the 1970s, 45 in the 1980s, 274 in the 1990s and 249 between the years 2000 and 2005. Although this increase is to some extent a product of the expansion of journal publishing, it also illustrates the growing influence of this concept in the social sciences. More important is the expansion of the usage of the term in relation to an expanding variety of groups and social experiences. It is worth noting that none of the six articles published in the 1950s used the concept vulnerability to refer to groups or people, but rather in association with the military and economic capabilities of countries and institutions. It is in the 1980s that the contemporary usage of the vulnerable as a defining feature of groups of people – the poor, elderly, mentally ill, minorities, children – is first evident. Since the 1990s the variety of experiences and types of people associated with the state of vulnerability by social scientists has steadily increased (International Bibliography of the Social Sciences, 1951-2005).

The conceptual inflation of vulnerable and vulnerability is also confirmed by research into the changing conceptualisation of childhood. Until the seventies, the social science literature tended to associate the response of children to adversity with their capacity for resilience. It was frequently argued that children were likely to respond to a disaster with resilience, especially if their family was able to serve as a source of social support (Block, Silber, and Perry 1956). However, 'about the middle of the 1970s the tone began to change as researchers began to scrutinise the matter more carefully' (Drabnek, 1986: 271). The main consequence of this new focus on children's mental health called into question the power of children's resilience and highlighted their vulnerability.

According to Frankenberg *et al* (2000), the tendency to frame children's problems through the metaphor of vulnerability is a relatively recent development. Their search of a major bibliographical database (BIDS) revealed over 800 refereed papers between 1986 and 1998 which focused on the relationship between vulnerability and children. They noted that 'whilst in the first four years of this period there were under ten references each year to vulnerability and children, an exponential increase to well over 150 papers a year occurred from 1990 onwards'. They believe that this figure underestimates the tendency to interpret children's lives through the prism of vulnerability since it ignores the substantial non-academic literature on the subject (Frankenberg *et al* 2000: 587).

A study of the emergence of the concept of vulnerable children shows that in most published literature the concept is treated 'as a relatively self-evident concomitant of childhood which requires little formal exposition'. It is 'considered to be an *essential* property of individuals, as something which is intrinsic to children's identities and personhoods, and which is recognisable through their beliefs and actions, or indeed through just their appearance' (*ibid*: 588-89). Vulnerability represents a statement about children's identity. It is also a cultural tool used for endowing childhood with meaning.

As an analytic concept, vulnerability does not entirely displace more socially oriented categories such as poverty, exploitation or discrimination. It merely flattens them out and re-represents them as a key dimension of daily experience of the human condition. This is a concept without boundaries. The past and the present are seamlessly connected through a chain of events whose cumulative outcome is a vulnerable community. The strong claims give it an almost indefinable metaphysical quality. De Chesnay points to its free-floating transcendental aspects:

> For some, the concept might be associated with people of colour or those who are socially marginalised. For others, it might evoke images of those who are poor, those who are frail, or those who are

without a voice. Vulnerability is equally at home with those who rely on others to speak for them, as it is with those who are homeless or disenfranchised. Vulnerability might extend to those who experience violence as part and parcel of human existence or those who go to bed hungry every night. (De Chesnay, 2005: xix)

And to underline the all inclusive character of the concept, De Chesnay adds that if we look at the 'private face of vulnerability, we might be surprised to see our own face'.

It is important to note that the concept of vulnerability did not emerge out of the experience of adversity. It is a term of description or a form of diagnosis that professionals adopt in their characterisation of communities. Even advocates of this concept concede that this is a term that outsiders use to label others. As Heijmans noted, vulnerability is not a 'concept that grassroots communities use'. She believes that 'vulnerability to disasters is a matter of perception, and in most aid agencies' perceptions, the view of local people is lacking'. Heijmans adds that 'most agencies tend to think on behalf of the victims, not realising that disaster-prone communities might interpret their circumstances differently' (Heijmans, 2001: 1, 15). It is well known that many communities that are diagnosed as vulnerable by aid agencies have 'no concept of 'vulnerability''. Indeed, in many 'local dialects, there is seldom an appropriate translation for the term' (*ibid*: 4). Even some proponents of the term recognise that the concept 'encourages a sense of societies and people as weak, passive and pathetic' (Bankoff, 2001: 29).

The vulnerability paradigm has emerged from a Western cultural imagination that possesses a feeble sense of human agency. The view is widely held that our era of 'globalisation', 'world risk society' and 'complexity' undermines people's capacity to exercise a sense of agency. This is expressed through what Melley describes as a 'sense of *diminished human agency*, a feeling that individuals cannot effect meaningful social action and, in extreme cases, may not be able to control their own behaviour' (Melley, 2001: 62). The constant tendency to inflate the conceptual status of vulnerability has led some researchers to raise questions about its promiscuous use: 'the word itself suffers from semantic overflow, since it refers to dependency or fragility as well as insecurity, centrality, complexity, the absence of effective regulation, gigantism, and low resilience' (Theys, 1985: 4).

Levine is concerned in the way that 'vulnerability stereotypes whole categories of individuals' and assumes that they are unable to 'know their best interests and to make appropriate choices for themselves' (2004: 399).

The ascendancy of the paradigm of vulnerability has little to do with its theoretical merit. Indeed it is precisely its general, diffuse, and all encompassing ambition that appeals to the imagination of the lay person and social scientist alike. According to one account, 'vulnerability is a useful general concept that depends on precise definition of events and context to provide useful insight into specific situations' (Kasperson and Kasperson, 2001: 26). Why it requires other more precise definitions of experience to be useful is far from evident. Its utility is not likely to be based on its analytical force but on its ability to express in a metaphor-like fashion an important cultural mood. Its proponents agree that it lacks focus and clarity: 'Although vulnerability is an intuitively simple notion, it is surprisingly difficult to define and even more difficult to quantify and operationalise' (Mohammad and Hossain, 2001: 16). The concept intuitively reflects a dimension of the cultural imagination. It works through successfully drawing on the vernacular resources of society: 'Perhaps vulnerability is not defined because its meaning seems self-evident' (Levine: 2004: 396). Indeed one reason why the term vulnerability is so rarely contested is because it thrives as a culturally affirmed ideal that social scientists use in a taken-for-granted way as does the lay public. Ewald (2002: 294) suggests that in recent times it has acquired the status of a 'sacred term' that illuminates taken-for-granted attitudes about the constitution of personhood.

The rhetorical appeal

Since the late 1970s the concept of vulnerability has migrated from ecology to the social sciences, particularly psychology where the term is often perceived as its very own invention (Scheid and Horwitz, 1999: 152). A concept oriented towards the analysis of personality traits was transformed into one also applied to groups. More importantly it was able to work idiomatically since its meaning corresponded to the common sense of the vernacular. A projection of an ecological scenario where individuals and their communities exist in a permanent state of vulnerability towards nature has been reframed through a therapeutic narrative to suggest that people's mental health is perpetually at risk from the uncertainties they face. As a rhetorical idiom, vulnerability is increasingly used to highlight the claim that people and communities lack the emotional and psychological resources necessary to engage with the challenges of everyday life.

The rhetorical appeal of vulnerability lies in its ability to capture the diffuse sense of individual powerlessness that prevails in 21st century Western societies. The ideals of self determination and autonomy are increasingly overridden by a more dominant message that emphasises the quality of human weakness (Furedi, 2005). That is why the idiom of vulnerability is habitually used as if it is a permanent feature of a person's biography. An advertisement for the post of Adult Protection Coordinator: 'protecting and empowering vulnerable adults is a priority in Greenwich' (*The Guardian*, 2005a) transmits the idea that there is a category of people called 'vulnerable adults' and that they require the protection of a paid professional. The ideals of child protection are imported into the provision of services for adults. The communicators of this idiom rarely ask the question 'vulnerable to what?' for the only answer they could give is: 'vulnerable to everything'.

Cultivating vulnerability

Claims made on behalf of the vulnerable attempt to cultivate modes of behaviour and attitudes that are bound up with this identity. Claims-making does not simply involve the demand for support and recognition; the construction of conditions that demand public attention 'often simultaneously construct the types of *people* who inhabit' such conditions (Loseke, 2003: 120). The idiom vulnerable should not be interpreted as merely a new word for the poor or the powerless. As a rhetorical idiom, it evokes a distinct approach towards the ideal of personhood and of human agency. Previous representation of the poor highlighted the socio-economic dimension of poverty. In contrast vulnerability is a psychological attribute that is bound up with the very meaning of contemporary personhood. It is integral to the consciousness through which people construct their reality. Ann Swidler observes that 'people vary greatly in how much culture they apply to their lives', but in the very act of using culture, people 'learn how to be, or become, particular kinds of persons. In this way people acquire a self-consciousness of what is expected of them and also about how they can expect to be treated (Swidler, 2001: 46, 71).

In addition, people's perception of vulnerability is influenced by the manner in which the term is cultivated by institutions, advocacy organisations, politicians and the media. Its ascendancy is founded upon the depoliticisation of inequality and the uneven distribution of resources (Furedi, 2005). This is a condition that people suffer and are powerless to alter. As Tremayne (2001: 16) noted, 'vulnerability is an all enveloping concept increasingly used by policy makers to describe situations in which people are either actually or potentially exposed to harm and are helpless to counteract it'. And 'because the vulnerable class cannot always 'help themselves" policy makers are entitled to speak on their behalf (Ibarra and Kistuse, 2003: 32). Often the idiom is used to transmit a powerful sense of passivity and even personal immaturity. The infantilisation of the vulnerable is integral to the strategy of protecting vulnerable adults. According to the official UK definition, a vulnerable adult is someone 'who is or may be in need of community care services by reason of mental or other disability, of age or illness; and who is or may be unable to take care of him or herself, or unable to protect him or herself against significant harm or exploitation' (Lord Chancellor's Department, 1997). Vulnerable adults are represented as biologically mature children who require official and professional support.

Precisely because it is beyond and above society, the rhetoric of vulnerability avoids engaging with the social, economic or political problems confronting the public. Helping or supporting the vulnerable has become a rhetorical device for legitimising a variety of diverse and unconnected causes and campaigns. Its internalisation into public discourse is symptomatic of the rise of self-consciously non-ideological centrist politics in the eighties. In both the UK and the US the embrace of the vulnerable coincided with attempts to depoliticise the issue of welfare entitlements and the provision of social services. Both sides of the debate – supporters of privatisation and their opponents – sought to champion the vulnerable to promote their cause. This development is linked to what Norman Fairclough (2000: 78) in his important discussion on New Labour's language has represented as the 'discourse of neo-liberalism'. It is part of the dominant political discourse but its rhetorical appeal is based on cultural influences that are wider than that, so the appeal of this word is no less potent among critics of 'neo-liberalism'.

In the 1980s, the cause of the vulnerable emerged as a *valence issue* (ie one that is unlikely to face opposition). For example, 'a valence issue such as child abuse elicits a single, strong, fairly uniform emotional response and does not have an adversarial quality', argues Nelson. Since no one can publicly claim to support child abuse, child protection advocates can appeal to a wide consensus. Interviewed policy makers repeatedly decried child abuse as a 'motherhood issue'. The two principal characteristics of valence issues are their lack of specificity and their vague affirmation of cultural values (Nelson, 1984: 26, 28). Consequently, support for the vulnerable is used as a rallying call by all sides of the political divide.

In UK newspapers, political criticisms of the Government, citing 'vulnerable groups', increased during the two year build up to the 1987 general election after which it became more common to mention the expression in relation to Government social policy. Critics of Prime Minister Margaret Thatcher frequently referred to the impact of her policies on the most vulnerable people in society. An article published in the *Financial Times* referred to the charge that the Government had 'failed to pay sufficient regard to health, education and preventive measures directed at the most vulnerable groups' (*The Financial Times*, 1987).

During the 1987 election campaign, the Labour Party often accused the Government's policies of hurting 'vulnerable groups' (*The Times*, 1987a). In reply, the Government also adopted this language, claiming that resources were being targeted at the most vulnerable groups. It is no surprise therefore, that during the bitter dispute over the poll tax, the cause of 'vulnerable groups' was supported by both the opposition and the British Government. In May 1987, the Government defended the poll tax by insisting that it protected 'the most vulnerable' (*The Times*, 1987b, *The Guardian*, 1987).

Since the late eighties, the lack of specificity of the usage of this term in official jargon has rarely been questioned by critics of the Government. A similar pattern is evident in the US. By the late eighties, both Democrats and the Republicans utilised the rhetoric of vulnerability. In 1987, the language of 'vulnerability' was adopted by the two main

Republican presidential contenders. Both Bush and Dole declared support for the vulnerable and sought to construct an image of 'compassionate' Republicanism (*The New York Times*, 1987).

The ability of the rhetoric of vulnerability to transcend the conventional ideological divide is symptomatic of the depoliticisation of public life (Furedi, 2005). Vulnerability has received cultural acclaim from social scientists, policy makers, politicians, and the media because it rests on taken for granted ideas and an emerging cultural narrative about the meaning of personhood. But the idiom of vulnerability did not simply spring from the popular imagination. It was developed, refined and applied by social scientists, advocacy organisations, and policy makers. Through its repetitive use, the sense of vulnerability was also cultivated and a new identity constructed. Understanding how all this shapes perceptions and attitudes towards private troubles and public problems constitutes an important challenge for those interested in confronting the language of power.

References

Aberdeen Press and Journal (2001) Lottery gets health drive up-and-running, 7th November

Bankoff, G (2001) Rendering the world unsafe: 'vulnerability' as western discourse. *Disasters* 25(1), p19-35

Best, J (1999) *Random Violence: how we talk about new crimes and new victims*. Berkeley, Ca: University of California Press

Block, D, Silber, E and Perry, S. (1956) Some factors in the emotional reaction of children to disasters. *American Journal of Psychiatry*, CX111, p416-22

Coventry Evening News (2005) The potential of a blind date can be worth all the pitfalls, 19th March

The Daily Mail (1997) We must care again for the vulnerable, 22nd May

The Daily Telegraph (2005a) On Easter Sunday, the world's most vulnerable lives hang in the balance, 27th March

The Daily Telegraph (2005b) Country diary, 15th October

De Chesnay, M (ed) (2005) *Caring For The Vulnerable: perspectives in nursing theory, practice and research*. Sudbury, Mass.: Jones and Bartlett Publishers

Drabnek, T (1986) *Human System Responses to Disaster: an inventory of sociological findings*. New York: Springer-Verlag

The Express (2000) The army of single dads struggling in silence, 7th September

Ewald, F (2002) The return of Descartes' malicious demon: an outline of a philosophy of precaution. In T Baker and J Simon (eds) *Embracing Risk: the changing culture of insurance and responsibility*. Chicago: University of Chicago Press

Fairclough, N (2000) *New Labour, New Language?* London: Routledge

The Financial Times (1987) The Thatcher years: divided they stand, 31st March

Frankenberg, R, Robinson, I and Delahooke, A (2000) Countering essentialism in behavioural social science: the example of the 'vulnerable child' ethnographically examined. *The Sociological Review* 48(4) p586-611

Furedi, F (2004) *Therapy Culture: cultivating vulnerability in an uncertain age.* London: Routledge

Furedi, F (2005) *The Politics of Fear: beyond left and right.* London: Continuum Press

Gergen, K (1990) Therapeutic professions and the diffusion of deficits, *The Journal of Mind and Behavior* 11(3) p353-368

The Guardian (1987) The day in politics: poll tax concession. 6th May

The Guardian (1995) Anger from charities at Straw blast on beggars: 'street cleaning is no way to deal with people who are vulnerable', 6th September

The Guardian (1998) Linked futures; grandparents: there are vulnerable groups at both ends of the age spectrum, 12th August

The Guardian (2004) Fear infects flexible workplaces, 2nd September

The Guardian (2005a) Utilities: national firms warned on cut-offs, 1st November

The Guardian (2005b) Carrying on the fight for workers' rights, 14th December

Heijmans, A (2001) Vulnerability: A Matter of Perception. Paper given at *International Work – conference on 'Vulnerability in Disaster theory and Practice'* organised by Wageningen Disaster Studies, 29th/30th June 2001

Ibarra, P and Kitsuse, J (2003) Claims-making discourse and vernacular resources. In J Holstein and G Miller (eds) *Challenges and Choices: constructionist perspectives on social problems.* New York: Aldine de Gruyter

The Independent (1994) Major accused of 'small-minded' attack on the most vulnerable, 30th May

The Independent (2000) Parents told to nurture a generation of boys who know it's ok to be vulnerable, 13th March

The Independent (2002) Making the abortion pill widely available is a sensible step, 8th July

The Independent (2003) One law for the rich, one for the vulnerable, 23rd March

International Bibliography of the Social Sciences (IBSS) (1951-present) available online @ http://ovidsp.uk.ovid.com/spb/ovidweb.cgi?New+Database=Single|4&S=IHCMPDFH AAHFGFDMFNILLBGHALPPAA00 accessed 6.2.08.

Kasperson, R, Kasperson, J and Dow, K (2001) Introduction. In J Kasperson and R Kasperson (eds) *Global Environmental Risk.* London: Earthscan

Levine, C (2004) The concept of vulnerability in disaster research. *Journal of Traumatic Stress* 17(5) p395-402

Lord Chancellor's Department (1997) *Who Decides? making decisions on behalf of mentally incapacitated adults.* London: HMSO

Loseke, D (2003) Constructing conditions, people, morality, and emotion: expanding the agenda of constructionism. In J Holstein and G Miller (eds) *Challenges and Choices: constructionist perspectives on social problems.* New York: Aldine de Gruyter

Melley, T (2001) Agency panic and the culture of conspiracy. In J Parish and M Parker (eds) *The Age of Anxiety: conspiracy theory and the human sciences.* Oxford: Blackwell Publishers

Mohammad, S and Hossain, N (2001) Assessing human vulnerability due to environmental change: concepts and assessment methodologies. Unpublished Master of Science Degree Thesis, Department of Civil and Environmental Engineering, Royal Institute of Technology, Stockholm

Nelson, B (1984) *Making An issue of Child Abuse: political agenda setting for social problems.* Chicago: University of Chicago Press

The New York Times (1969) The panel urges changes in FTC, 16th September

The New York Times (1987) Presidential politics: compassion becomes a Republican theme, 22nd October

The New York Times (1998) Is Big Brother watching? Why would he bother? We're all vulnerable, 12th January

The New York Times (2005) The vulnerable become more vulnerable, 2nd January

The Observer (2003) Dangerous pursuit of beauty: the media's notion that thinness is next to godliness plays havoc with vulnerable young minds, 9th November

Scheid, L and Horwitz, A (1999) The social context of mental health in A Horwitz and T Scheid (eds) *Handbook for the Study of Mental Health: social contexts, theories and systems*. Cambridge: Cambridge University Press

The Sunday Express (2005) Should digital TV be given out free? Express debate, 23rd October

The Sunday Telegraph (2004) Still gazing at the stars, 12th December

Swidler, A (2001) *Talk of Love: how culture matters*. Chicago: The University of Chicago Press

Theys, J (1985) La société vulnérable. In J-L Fabiani and J Theys (eds) *La Société Vulnérable: évaluer et maîtriser les risques*. Paris : Presses de l'Ecole Normale Supérieure

The Times (1968) Mothers on their own, 22nd November

The Times (1973) Saving the housebound, 16th January

The Times (1974) Minorities the most vulnerable and the most difficult to help, 21st May

The Times (1987a) Tebbit denounces spoof manifesto, 29th April

The Times (1987b) Parliament: aid promised on rates bill, 6th May

The Times (2002) Rowan Williams, 4th December

Tremayne, S (ed) (2001) *Managing Reproductive Life: cross cultural themes in fertility*. New York: Berghahn Books

Williams, G and Williams, R (1995) 'All we want is equality': rhetorical framing in the fathers' rights movement. In J Best (ed) *Images of Issues*. Hawthrone, NY: Aldine de Gruyter

4

Risky Research or Researching Risk: the role of ethics review

PAT SIKES AND HEATHER PIPER

Introduction

This chapter discusses our attempts to gain institutional permission to investigate school teachers' perceptions and experiences of being 'falsely'[1] accused of sexually abusing students and also our attempts to obtain funding to enable us to do so. We discuss the difficulties encountered which, we suggest, result from our attempt to research a topic which comes within the ambit of the contemporary moral panic around paedophilia and child abuse. Undoubtedly, studies which deal with controversial and/or sensitive areas can have personal and professional implications and consequences for the researchers involved in them (Sikes, 2006a; 2006b, *in press*) and negotiating university ethical review bodies has increasingly become recognised as an issue of substantial significance for all researchers. Referring to the proliferation in recent years of journal articles and books discussing Institutional Review Boards (IRBs) and other procedures of ethical review, Halse and Honey go so far as to talk about the 'crescendo of angst amongst researchers about the governing practices of research ethics' (2007: 341). This angst is generally occasioned by what often appears to be, and is experienced as, the curtailment of academic freedom in the interests of protecting universities against, *inter alia*, legal challenges, perceived loss of academic and research related status, and association with socially unacceptable beliefs, practices and values (see, for instance, Tierney and Blumberg Corwin, 2007). Our account begins with some background information about our proposed research before we discuss the moral panic around child abuse; ethics committees; our experiences with ethics committees; and, more briefly, our experiences with potential funders.

Background

Using remarkably similar language, successive Secretaries of State for Education and Skills responsible for policy and provision in England and Wales have commented that:

> ... sometimes the facts show that allegations are not true [yet] once the allegations have been made, whether they are true or not, a life may be ruined. (Estelle Morris, 2001)

> I am very much aware of the devastating effect that false or unfounded allegations can have on a teacher's health, family and career. The length of time it takes to investigate an allegation and the surrounding publicity can make its impact so much more severe. (Charles Clarke, 2004)

> I am very much aware of the devastating effect that being wrongly or unfairly accused can have on an individual, their family and their career. (Ruth Kelly, 2006) (All above quoted in Revell, 2007)

These statements acknowledge that, in England and Wales at least, false allegations are made against teachers. Indeed, there is evidence to suggest that the incidence of such allegations is rising (NASUWT, 2003; Revell, 2007).

As a result of personal knowledge of teachers who had been falsely accused of sexual misconduct against pupils, and on the basis of previous research which addressed teachers' fears of touching their pupils in which one of us had been involved (Piper, Stronach and MacLure, 2006; Piper and Stronach, 2008 forthcoming), we regarded this as an area that called out for investigation. Preliminary enquiries revealed that, contrary to what usually happens in cases of alleged sexual assault, accused teachers are publicly named. We learnt that in many instances, once an allegation is made, teachers are suspended or prohibited from working with pupils. Even though, 'in employee relations terms, suspension is deemed a neutral act' (DfES, 2004a: 2), that 'is in itself not a disciplinary measure' (Myers *et al*, 2005: 95), the legalistic human resources rhetoric does not usually match the perceptions or experiences of those involved. The fact that allegations have been made often produces a presumption of guilt, and 'once reported, the staff involved are forbidden to discuss the case with anyone' (*ibid*: 117). It is recognised that the anxiety caused is such that 'frequently (*investigatory*) proceedings will be interrupted by the stress and ill health of the teacher concerned', and 'capability procedures relating to ill health may, in some circumstances, supersede the disciplinary process' (*ibid*: 99).

The fallout or collateral damage from this 'neutral' process is far-reaching and sometimes tragic. Many facing false allegations cannot sustain family relationships, have breakdowns, and cannot return to the classroom when their ordeal is over. Statistics show that a 'significant number of people resign after an allegation is made against them' regardless of the veracity of the accusation (DfES, 2004b: 2.11), and there have been cases of suicide (NASUWT, 2004; Revell, 2007). In one case a male teacher, Darryl Gee, died in prison four years into an eight year sentence and four years before he was posthumously acquitted. Thus, careers and lives are ruined and experienced professionals are lost. Furthermore, the principles of natural justice are clearly being contravened in that people are presumed guilty prior to full and impartial investigation. Even when later cleared through investigation, they frequently continue to bear the stigma of a 'spoilt identity' (Goffman, 1963).

We developed a proposal for a project whose overall aim was to explore teachers' perceptions of these experiences. Our intention was that the project would engage with the range of individuals who are touched by any accusation (the accused, their family, friends, colleagues, senior staff) and that it would take a narrative, auto/biographical approach involving the collection of multi-layered accounts (via interviews, questionnaires, documentary analysis). On the basis of findings, we hoped to be able to offer recommendations for policy and practice. We were well aware that any project involving sex and children was likely to be problematic. In this case the inevitable sensitivity was heightened by: potentially giving voice to people who had indeed abused children and who were seeking to hide this behind a claim of false allegations; and the way in which, in the contemporary climate, questioning a) whether child abuse has occurred, and/or b) the nature of procedures and practices set up to deal with it, are both seen by some to be abusive.

Moral Panic around Child Abuse

Moral panic has been defined as: 'A reaction by a group of people based on the false or exaggerated perception that some cultural behaviour or group, frequently a minority group or subculture, is dangerously deviant and poses a menace to society' (Wikipedia, nd). The term was first used in connection with the mods and rockers phenomenon of 1960s Great Britain (Cohen, 1972) but, throughout history, it also effectively describes responses to, *inter alia*, witches, Jews and gypsies. Currently there is a state of moral panic around children and their vulnerability (see for example McWilliam and Jones, 2005; Piper and Smith, 2003). Murphy (2005) describes moral panic as a form of 'new Puritanism' which can lead to behaviour likened to the witch-hunts of previous centuries and to collective fantasies and moral crusades seeking to 'purify the world through the annihilation of some category of human beings imagined as agents of corruption and incarnations of evil' (Webster, 2005: xv). Paedophiles are currently cast in this light and anyone who is for any reason suspected or accused of such tendencies and behaviours is likely to be subject to the full force of social loathing, disgust, and demonisation (Wilson, 1990). To note this is not of course to say that paedophiles do not exist, nor that they are not dangerous. Indeed, 'there should be no doubt that child sexual abuse is one of the most serious social problems of our age, and that it is more widespread than many people are prepared to accept' (Webster, 2005: 537). An essential characteristic of a moral panic however, is that people who are not in fact witches or paedophiles are wrongly identified as such and treated as if they were.

The sexually abused child has become an integral element of the iconography of Anglophone culture (Scott, in Piper and Stronach 2008 forthcoming). What is considered to constitute abuse covers a wide spectrum involving actual behaviours, perceptions and intentions, and establishing that abuse has taken place is not always easy. Estimates of the actual occurrence of child abuse are usually retrospective (ie child protection charities asking a sample of adults whether they were abused as children), and vary according to the definition of abuse applied, from one in ten to one in four. In response, an 'industry' (Furedi, 2001; Scott, 2003) exists to detect and prevent this abuse. For instance, in the UK and elsewhere, anyone who is expected to come into contact with children is subjected to a vetting procedure (see DfES, 2006). The belief in the existence of numerous opportunistic sexual predators has shaped legislation and many adults now police their own behaviours accordingly. However, it has been authoritatively suggested that 80 per cent of child abusers are biological parents (eg UNICEF, http://www.unicef.org.uk/press/news_detail.asp?news_id=180). If abuse by step-parents is added to this figure, it leaves a relatively small percentage of abuse that can be attributed to the 'stranger', and even less to professionals, such as teachers, acting in *loco parentis*.

Ethics Committees

Ethics committees whose responsibilities include addressing potential and/or actual ethical dilemmas in research are not new (see, *inter alia*, Bulmer, 1982; Burgess, 1984; Simons and Usher, 2000). However, more recently others (Halse and Honey, 2007; Sikes, in press) have suggested that ethics committees are not merely concerned with addressing moral dilemmas, but now increasingly act as gatekeepers, with their chief concern being the avoidance of litigation. Referring specifically to consent forms, but with equal relevance to ethics committees, Fine and her co-authors (2000) go as far as to suggest they can be invoked to absolve researchers from their moral and ethical responsibilities. A further difficulty relates to the ways in which ethics committees tend to be governed by principles inclining towards scientific, biomedical models of objective, experimental inquiry, and an essentialised view of human beings and human nature. For example, medical research ethics committees have traditionally acted in accordance with such beliefs and medical guidelines and frameworks based on this premise have been enshrined in governmental documentation (see DoH 2001). Such beliefs take for granted that reason leads to truth, and that rules are required in order to rationalise and justify all moral choices (Beauchamp *et al*, 1982).

Common to these approaches is what Dawson (1994) referred to as an 'outside-in' view of human nature, where it is assumed that individuals, left to their own devices, are likely to make wild judgements. Thus, they need taming through the application of guidelines which will provide answers to moral and ethical problems in advance. To behave properly, individuals merely have to follow the rules. Like Fine *et al* (2000), Dawson claimed that ethical codes are in reality unethical as they minimise an individuals' responsibility for their actions and therefore stand in the way of moral development. Pring (2000) also notes that each research situation generates its own ethical questions and issues that demand unique and contextual answers. Social and educational research ethics committees in the UK and elsewhere are currently following the medical blueprint, and universities (following directives from research councils eg ESRC, 2005) are encouraging a proliferation in the number and power of ethics committees.

Scott (2003) has critiqued the recent development of ethics committees and in particular the 'obsession' that research participants must give informed consent to their involvement in the research process, and in addition be able to satisfy the researcher and the ethics committee that they have done so. She argues that this practice, in essence, places research participants on a par with vulnerable children who cannot truly consent without the guidance of those who know better, since with the introduction of the notion of consent comes a shift in responsibility. If a research participant has consented to something then any ill-effects become their own responsibility. Research participants are primarily considered to be potential litigants who may sue if they can claim some harm has resulted from their involvement in the research process. As a result, researchers are now managed in ways which would have scarcely been credible a few decades ago (*ibid*), and university managers and administrators have found ethics committees to be a useful way to control researchers who previously enjoyed autonomy in their work (*ibid*; O'Brien, 2006). Ethics committees thus function against the backdrop of anxiety and their effects have provided a successful way of increasing the surveillance and control of both researchers and research participants.

Our Experiences with Ethics Committees[2]

It is common now in all universities in the UK for affiliated staff and student researchers who are intending to do any research which involves human participants in any way (directly or indirectly) to have their proposal approved by an ethics committee, before they can proceed with empirical work. This is often justified in terms of it helping to protect the dignity, rights, safety and well-being of participants and researchers. In our experience the process begins with applicants completing a form which asks for information regarding their project's aims and objectives; the methodology and methods they intend to employ; how participants are to be identified and contacted; what measures will be taken to ensure confidentiality of personal data; whether informed consent will be sought; if there is potential for any physical or psychological harm to participants; whether payment will be made, and if there are any issues relating to the safety of researchers. This form is then sent out to reviewers: two in the case of research undertaken as part of a student assignment and three when it is doctoral or staff research. The idea that students require less surveillance than more experienced staff is in itself somewhat surprising. Reviewers are asked to indicate whether, in their view, the application should be approved, be approved providing specified requirements are met, or should not be approved for reasons which must be stated. Only if there is unanimous agreement is the researcher free to continue. In the case of approval being denied by one or more reviewers, the Chair of the Departmental Ethics Review Panel adjudicates. If the situation is complex or controversial and/or the reasons for refusal are serious, the Chair may seek advice and/or refer the case to the University level ethics committee. A further application is usually then sought.

In line with requirements we completed an ethics review application. This was sent out to the statutory three reviewers. A month later we received notification that our proposal had not been approved. One reviewer, for whom we provide the pseudonym Sue, expressed the view, similar to that taken by the DfES that 'fortunately, cases of malicious allegations or false allegations that are wholly invented are very rare' (DfES, 2004b: 2.9). However, as neither the DfES, nor Sue, cite research evidence to support this claim and, given the negative tenor of her other comments, we were left wondering how best to proceed.

The idea that children never lie about abuse was promoted some 20 or more years ago when, in the UK and USA (and elsewhere), a number of cases of ritual and/or satanic abuse came to trial, often on the basis of medical 'evidence', and, for the most part (albeit after a lengthy period of time), dismissed (Webster, 2005: 88-94). Such truisms that lump all children and young people together appear problematic in any consideration of specific examples. While it is certainly unlikely that a 4 year old could describe incest in detail if they had not experienced it, the idea that a 15 year old who is angry with one of their teachers is incapable of falsehood is far less plausible. Sue appeared to be saying that the only valid argument for allowing us to continue with the research was for us to present a body of research evidence already available – that very same research her objections had been instrumental in delaying, if not prohibiting. Sue also found difficulty with our usage of quotation marks around the word 'falsely' in our title, suggesting that it could, in the future, be upsetting to youngsters who had made allegations which had resulted in convictions, and to those children who had witnessed actual abusers being acquitted.

Sue seemed to take a view which did not accept that an accusation could be false. Any evidence that we had cited in our proposal was also apparently discounted, since the paramountcy of the child ('the child' being in the abstract and general) was all that mattered. On this view, distress caused to anyone who may have been falsely accused is seen as subservient to the possible distress of a young person. It is significant to note that the ethics review procedure which researchers must satisfy is said to be there to protect research participants (and researchers): in our case specific teachers who have been accused. However, it seemed to us that we were being taken to task for failing to protect unknown and, most significantly, hypothetical children who were to play no part in the research process.

A number of potential solutions were offered. For instance, it was suggested that we exclude people who had been found guilty from our sample. In other words we had to accept that court hearings had only one outcome: the truth. This confidence in the legal system meant that, in effect, we would need to leave out the very people we were most keen to include. Those who find themselves in a similar situation to Darryl Gee (see above) would have had to be excluded from our sample.

Sue was later invited (by the Chair of the Departmental Review Panel) to explain her concerns in more detail in writing. This communication made it clear that Sue had experience of the field of child protection, and the discourse of false acquittal that she employed further supported the supposition that false allegations are extremely rare. It is worth remembering here that the whole language of child abuse over the past 20-30 years has been premised on the notion that a child who makes an accusation must in the first instance be believed, which has been re-scripted to mean a child never lies about child abuse. This has been noted by others who have remarked that referring to children 'making disclosures' is also a form of words which presupposes guilt (Butler-Sloss, 1988).

Additionally Sue noted her commitment to a child-centred approach in line with the previously mentioned legal and paramount principle of the welfare of the child. This is contentious since, although an accurate interpretation of the Children Act, it nevertheless raises questions as to the paramountcy of other vulnerable groups (the elderly, severely disabled etc), not to mention other members of society presumed to be less important in such an analysis. In the case of our research, the falsely accused are just such a vulnerable group and are, we believe, deserving of attention to their well-being.

We have no doubt that Sue undertook her responsibilities as an ethics reviewer with seriousness and with the intention to be fair and just, both to potential informants and to us as fellow researchers. However, in our opinion and on the basis of the evidence available to us it seems that the way in which the procedure operates led Sue to adopt a regulatory role, casting her as a protector of the young and innocent, and her actions, if not her intentions, lead us to the conclusion that she considered us as researchers at best naïve and at worst dangerous. (It is perhaps worth noting here that one of us has a similar background to the reviewer in child protection work, and is experienced in interviewing abused children and their abusers.) This impression was further strengthened by negative comments relating to our plan to seek advice from FACT – a national association for 'Falsely Accused Carers and Teachers' (see www.factuk.org) which has considerable parliamentary and high ranking legal practitioner support. These comments, in our view, implied that we were incapable of acting independently from any group we may include as part of our research sample.

Sue did conclude her feedback by expressing the difficulties she experienced in commenting on a proposal that was so closely related to, and intimately bound up with, her work and with strongly held beliefs, values and commitments. She speculated on whether or not this might constitute a conflict of interest. Had this conflict been taken into account and had Sue been withdrawn from the process at the start, we would have been able to proceed with the research, since neither of the other two reviewers said that the work should not be approved. Bearing this in mind, the Departmental Panel Chair advised us to resubmit.

Our second attempt to gain approval fell foul of further concerns and demands from a fresh batch of reviewers. We were advised that: 'the [researchers] need to state clearly and in sufficient detail how confidentiality and/or anonymity will be protected' (although we believed we had done this); also that there was a 'lack of detail regarding how informed consent will be obtained' (although this was clearly stated); and 'more detail is needed on what procedures will be followed to ensure that the researcher's personal safety won't be put at risk' etc. Such demands had not been made the first time the proposal was considered, and it is our view that they reflect little confidence in us as researchers. They also suggest that our previous relevant experience appears to be counted for naught. There is of course an implicit assumption (although, no doubt, this could be disputed) in all of these statements that ethics committees exist to regulate and prevent any research that could be described in any way as sensitive or, perhaps more importantly, as risky. However (and even though subsequent attempts to secure funding were also unsuccessful – see below) we have not given up with our intention to pursue this research. Finally we learnt that our third submission had been given university approval.

Our Experiences with Potential Funders

Whilst the story we have been concerned to tell here is primarily one of our, or more precisely our potential research project's, relationship with ethical review committees, our experiences of trying to obtain funding are also pertinent because in many respects the problems were similar.

We have applied to three sources: the ESRC (Economic Social and Research Council), a teachers' union, and a general research fund competitively available to staff in the institution where one of us works. On each occasion we have been unsuccessful. Of course, it could simply be that our proposals have been weak. However, the limited feedback we have received together with our experiences around obtaining ethical clearance lead us to believe that our rejections are worthy of further consideration. We were under no illusion that we would easily gain financial support for our work. Nevertheless, because the government had expressed concern about the rising incidence of false allegations (DfES, 2004c), and since the teachers' unions were actively seeking to find ways of protecting their members (eg NASUWT, 2004; Revell, 2007), we felt this was an area with funding potential. We have a number of referees' rejection reports from each of the potential funders approached.

Comments about our theoretical approach and proposed methodology and our capability to undertake the project were all generally positive and all reviewers agreed that this was an important area to investigate. One reviewer did raise questions about 'issues with reliability and validity with respect to the account elicited' and suggested that 'it might be valuable to consider in what ways the analysis might be deficient should the accounts and perspectives of accusers themselves not be included in the study'. Another wrote, 'one area of concern is the limited consideration to be given to the motives of accusers, and the way in which they construct their accusations'. The suggestion here seems to be that a) we should be seeking to establish 'truth', in a judicial sort of a way, and also that we should interview children who have been found to have made false allegations. Whilst we had considered the possibility of doing this, we eventually decided against it because of the potential distress it could cause. In the light of the views of Sue, the ethics reviewer we quoted extensively from earlier, who was concerned lest some anonymous child be upset should they come across our work, this seems ironic.

However, what we consider to be particularly interesting about our failure to secure funding are the following comments, each of which comes from a different, anonymous, reviewer:

- The researchers should perhaps not underestimate the strength of likely negative media comment

■ This is seen as a courageous proposal, but ... this would be a high risk study.

■ This is a promising project but it does raise issues

■ ... the researchers may find that they collude with both the university and the alleged abuser into keeping quiet about the issues raised by research such as this, or alternatively, they may not be able to control the media through a sympathetic journalist ...

These reviewers were concerned about the difficulties associated with the area and what the media might make of it. So were we. Neither of us are strangers to the sort of controversy that can be engendered by research linking school students, teachers and sex (see Sikes, 2006b) or to managing controversy resulting from research more broadly (Piper, 2003). Accordingly we had talked about how to address potential problems in our proposal. Indeed, one reviewer acknowledged this: 'The researchers are aware of the difficulties of dissemination in this sensitive area including possible media interpretations or 'sensationalising'. These are genuine concerns but they should not prevent research in this area', however, this is exactly what they have done!

Concluding Remarks

We live in a society ruled by a culture of fear, where perceived (and imagined) risks far outweigh the likelihood of that which is feared actually happening (Pieterman, 2001), but where, nevertheless, lives are ordered and policed to protect against any sort of potential occurrence (see Beck, 1992; Castel, 1999; Furedi, 1997). In this context, taking risks is often not allowed, and would-be risk takers can be silenced. This is the sort of society which, we believe, led to our negative experience with the ethics review procedure and funding applications. Our concern here is with the surveillance and control of research and academic freedom and voice. Plummer (1995) has written that 'now the time has certainly come for personal sexual stories to be told', and then adds the caveat, 'at least for some groups' (*ibid*: 6). He was taking a general perspective regarding which and whose stories are deemed acceptable within the public arena. In the more specific context of stories told under the heading of research, it seems to us that ethical review committees are playing an increasingly significant role in validating the kinds of stories and accounts which are to be accorded some status as truths (see Lincoln, 2005).

We have already suggested that protecting against possible litigation is one of the functions of ethics committees, and safeguarding institutions is undoubtedly often a major concern. However, such caution, a consequence of the technologisation and institutionalisation of research ethics (see Halse and Honey, 2007), may do little to advance the development of critical and innovative research which could result in social justice outcomes. In contrast it could lead to researchers playing safe or even in some cases leaving the academy (see Foley and Valenzuela, 2005; Sikes, 2006c). We believe that, as academics, we have a responsibility to act as public intellectuals (Goodson, 1997; and see also the chapter by Fazal Rizvi), to raise difficult questions and to investigate areas that are sensitive and difficult. Such a contribution appears to be increasingly problematic.

But there is another issue at play here too, one which is particularly ironic given that our research concerns false accusations. Halse and Honey suggest that 'the practices and protocols for ethics approval are vulnerable to scripting researchers and research 'subjects' in binary terms' (2007: 246), as 'us' and 'them'. Given that the primary, avowed purpose of ethics review is to protect research subjects, the assumption has to be that they need protecting from dangerous researchers or researchers who are 'morons' (as Tierney and Blumberg Corwin, 2007: 396, put it). Like the teachers whose experiences and perceptions we wanted to research, we too have had to prove ourselves innocent, having been presumed to be guilty, if only of incompetence. Such an approach is preventing rather than facilitating educational and social research. Nonetheless we do believe that our intended topic is an important area about which insufficient is known. Its significance goes beyond the blighted lives and experience of those falsely accused, and touches on the nature and possibility of professional practice and engagement in a risk society.

Notes

1   We know that not all who claim false accusation are telling the truth. However, to simplify reading we have refrained forthwith from placing quotation marks around the words false and falsely throughout, even when their usage may have warranted it.

2   The wording and detail of this and related sections are significantly different from the version that we originally wrote. Prior to the final submission of the text, we were put under extreme pressure (applied by individuals and institutional sources) to make radical changes which, in our view, softened our critique. The difficulties we experienced add further weight to the arguments we advance here – indeed they deserve to become a story in its own right.

References

Beauchamp, T, Faden, R, Wallace, R and Walters, L (1982) (eds) *Ethical Issues in Social Science Research*. Baltimore: John Hopkins University Press

Beck, U (1992) *Risk Society: towards a new modernity*. London: Sage

Bulmer, M (1982) (ed) *Social research ethics: an examination of the merits of covert participant observation*. London: Macmillan

Burgess, R (1984) *In the field: an introduction to field research*. London: Allen and Unwin

Butler-Sloss, E (1988) *Report of the Inquiry into Child Abuse in Cleveland 1987*. London: HMSO

Castel, R (1999) From dangerousness to risk. In G Burchell, C Gordon and P Miller (eds) *The Foucault Effect: studies in governmentality*. Chicago: University of Chicago Press

Cohen, S (1972) *Folk Devils and Moral Panics*. London: MacGibben and Kee

Dawson, A (1994) Professional codes of practice and ethical conduct. *Journal of Applied Philosophy* 11(2) p145-153

DfES (2004a) *Staff Subject to Allegations: thresholds for and alternatives to suspension*. London: DfES

DfES (2004b) *Proposals for Dealing with Allegations against Teachers and Other Staff: a consultation*. London: DfES

DfES (2004c) '*Walking Tall*' – More Support For Schools to Tackle Bad Behaviour. http://www.dfes.gov.uk/pns/DisplayPN.cgi?pn_=2004_0196 (accessed 9th August 2007)

DfES (2006) *Safeguarding Vulnerable Groups Act 2006*, London: Department for Education and Skills.

DoH (2001) (revised 2005) *Research Governance Framework for Health and Social Care*, London: Department of Health.

ESRC (2005) *Research Ethics Framework*, Swindon: Economic and Social Research Council.

Fine, M, Weiss, L, Wessen, S and Wong, L (2000) For whom? Qualitative research, representations and social responsibilities. In N Denzin and Y Lincoln (eds) *The Handbook of Qualitative Research, 2nd edition*. Thousand Oaks, Ca: Sage

Foley, D and Valenzuela, A (2005) Critical ethnography: the politics of collaboration. In N Denzin and Y Lincoln (eds) *The Sage Handbook of Qualitative Research, 3rd edition*. Thousand Oaks, Ca: Sage

Furedi, F (1997) *Culture of Fear*. London: Cassell

Furedi, F (2001) *Paranoid Parenting*. London: Allen Lane

Furedi, F (2002) *The culture of fear: risk-taking and the morality of low expectation, 2nd edition*. London: Continuum

Goffman, E (1963) *Stigma: notes on the management of a spoilt identity*. Englewood Cliffs, NJ: Prentice Hall

Goodson, I (1997) The educational researcher as a public intellectual. The Lawrence Stenhouse Memorial Lecture, British Educational Research Association, University of York

Halse, C and Honey, A (2007) Rethinking ethics review as institutional discourse. *Qualitative Inquiry* 13(3) p336-352

Lincoln, Y (2005) Institutional review boards and methodological conservatism: the challenge to and from phenomenological paradigms. In N Denzin and Y Lincoln (eds) *The Sage Handbook of Qualitative Research, 3rd edition*. Thousand Oaks, Ca: Sage

McWilliam, E and Jones, A (2005) An unprotected species? On teachers as risky subjects. *British Educational Research Journal* 31(1) p109-120

Murphy, J (2005) The assault of pleasure: is a new Puritanism on the march? *Spiked e journal*, 11.8.05

Myers, K with Clayton, G, James, D and O'Brien, J (2005) *Teachers Behaving Badly: dilemmas for school leaders*. London: Routledge/Falmer

NASUWT (24/4/03) Campaign to Protect Teachers from Malicious Allegations. http://www.teachersunion.org.uk/Templates/internal.asp?NodeID=69333 (accessed 16th July 2006)

NASUWT (9/6/04) NASUWT Petition for Anonymity for Teachers facing Malicious Allegations to be presented to House of Commons. http://www.teachersunion.org.uk/Templates/internal.asp?NodeID=70839 (accessed 16th July 2006)

O'Brien, R (2006) The institutional review board problem: where it came from and what to do about it. *Journal of Social Distress and the Homeless* XV(1) p24-46

Pieterman, R (2001) Culture in the risk society: an essay on the rise of a precautionary culture. *Zeitschrift für Rechtssoziologie* 22(2) p145-168

Piper, H (2003) The linkage of animal abuse with interpersonal violence: a sheep in wolf's clothing? *Journal of Social Work* 3(2) p161-177

Piper, H and Smith, H (2003) Touch in educational and child care settings: dilemmas and responses. *British Educational Research Journal* 29(6) p879-894

Piper, H and Stronach, I (2008) *Don't Touch! An educational story of a panic*. London: Routledge

Piper, H, Stronach, I and MacLure, M (2006) *Touchlines: the problematics of touching between professionals and children*. ESRC – RES-000-22-0815

Plummer, K (1995) *Telling Sexual Stories: power, change and social worlds*. London: Routledge

Pring, R (2000) *Philosophy of Educational Research*. London: Continuum

Revell, P (2007) Guilty by Accusation: a research paper presented for discussion at the NAHT Conference. Paper presented at the NAHT Conference, Bournemouth

Simons, H and Usher, R (2000) *Situated Ethics in Educational Research*. London: Routledge/Falmer

Scott, C (2003) Ethics and knowledge in the contemporary university. *Critical Reviews in International Social and Political Philosophy* 6(4) p93-107

Sikes, P (2006a) On dodgy ground? Problematics and ethics in educational research. *International Journal of Research and Method in Education* 29(1) p105-117

Sikes, P (2006b) A cautionary tale concerning journalists and moral panic. *Research Intelligence* 95 p4-6

Sikes, P (2006c) Towards useful and dangerous theories. Discourse: *Studies in the Cultural Politics of Education* 27(1) p43-51.

Tierney, W and Blumberg Corwin, Z (2007) The tensions between academic freedom and institutional review boards. *Qualitative Inquiry* 13(3) p388-398

Webster, R (2005) *The Secret of Bryn Estyn: the making of a modern witchhunt*. Oxford: Orwell Press

Wikipedia (nd) Moral Panic. http://en.wikipedia.org/wiki/Moral_panic (accessed May 2007)

Wilson, E (1990) Immoral Panics. *New Statesman and Society*, 31.8.90

5

Whose Truth? Whose (Who's In) Power? International development, qualitative methodologies and science in Central America

SUSAN HEALD

Introduction

Beginning from the feminist insight that oppressions and inequalities are interlocking, and which are salient in any given interaction is a matter for analysis, I attempt here to make sense of a 'development' project with which I was briefly involved. The paper is about a course which I was supposed to, but did not, teach in Central America. But since the reason it will not be taught are related to the reasons it needed to be taught in the first place, I decided to write about the course I would have taught and tie it to a critique of development and much other trans-national or cross-cultural work.

The course was called 'Qualitative Methodologies for Investigating Community Knowledge, Power and Gender,' and was to be offered as part of a six-year, million-dollar university partnerships project funded by the Canadian International Development Agency (CIDA) and initiated by a faculty member in Soil Science. The project was meant to link the universities of Manitoba and Costa Rica. Also involved were the National Agrarian University of Nicaragua and the

La Ceiba campus of the National Autonomous University of Honduras. However, the status of the latter two was always ambiguous. In the initial design, the linkage was strictly between Manitoba and Costa Rica, but CIDA politics led to Honduras and Nicaragua being added. My sense that they were not really considered equal partners became one of the axes of conflict for the project initiator/director and me. I was asked to be involved by the Canadian project director after a letter of intent was approved, in time to make a trip to Costa Rica, Nicaragua, and Honduras, ostensibly to develop the full proposal. Along the way I learned that I was the only member of the three-person Canadian team who knew any Spanish, that the project director had spent a total of two weeks in Central America, that Costa Ricans tend to hold extremely condescending views towards other Central Americans, especially Nicaraguans, and that the other Canadian and Costa Rican team members were comfortable with a model in which the Costa Ricans were situated as the teachers of the others, a model I considered imperialist.

The background I brought to the project included extensive work in Latin America, beginning in Colombia 30 years ago and focused in Nicaragua for over fifteen years. My work in Nicaragua has primarily been with a new university on the Caribbean Coast (URACCAN) including an earlier partnership project working with URACCAN on *capacitación* of the university's human resources. Most recently, my work with URACCAN involves teaching a biannual course for Canadian students, in which they travel to Nicaragua to learn from scholars and activists in the region and to work in partnership with URACCAN students on small research projects about various aspects of *costeña* women's lives.

This work, combined with reading and teaching feminist, antiracist, postcolonial and post-structural literature on theories, methodologies and pedagogies, led me to a set of political, methodological, epistemological and pedagogical practices. The bulk of my academic energies in the past decade or more have gone into struggling through these words-on-paper to positions which would serve my work with both Canadian and Nicaraguan students, all the while adjusting these positions in the light of lessons learned through experience. For example, in my initial moment of negotiating the work I would do with URACCAN, was to say that I did not want to teach because teaching, it seemed to me, was, in this context, hopelessly imperialist. But, my new Nicaraguan colleague replied, teaching is what we need you to do.

So there I was, having to decide whether it was more imperialist to teach or to claim that my Nicaraguan colleagues were unable to decide what was good for them and so it was up to me to override their desires! I taught. Yet in the university partnerships project I have outlined above, I did not teach. The difference lay not in the distance between the Central American agronomists and me, but between me and the Canadian soil scientists. Although my abstract positions have been challenged through the years, I still insist that all interactions between people need to involve a critique of development, acknowledging the ways development is built on imperialist notions of Western superiority in the realms of, at least, economics, technology, politics, knowledge and culture, all of which are intensely racialised and gendered. In the next section, I sketch out just three components of such a critique.

Three elements of a critique of development

The first can be summed up as putting solidarity before charity. The receiver of charity can never stand in a relationship of equality with the giver. Further, it is usually the giver who gets to decide what will be given; the receiver is left to be grateful. This stance has been complicated throughout my work at URACCAN. For example, in the context of my bringing the Canadian students to learn from Costeña faculty, students and community workers, I have come to see it only appropriate that the students and I should find ways to give something back in return for the generous gifts of time and knowledge we receive. As it turns out, what my colleagues from URACCAN say they want in return are ideas about research methods and a research agenda for themselves. While I still feel the need to tread cautiously in terms of what we can offer and how we should offer it, this in no way seems to me to be charity. Relations can be reciprocal, but only when attention to the always readily-available charity model is constant and reflexive.

Secondly, every situation needs to be analysed to uncover the ways it is inflected with, at least, gender and race. One of the worst legacies of liberalism, still being handed down to generation after generation of Western children who grow up to become our students in universities, is the idea that racism and sexism have been bypassed and, further, that this has been accomplished by ignoring them. To admit the existence of race and gender, even as socially-constructed categories, is to acknowledge that you *notice* and, in noticing, therefore automatically accede to racist and sexist beliefs. Being gender-neutral or non-sexist, and colour-blind or non-racist are seen to be the solutions.

Feminist and critical race scholars have shown that both pedagogy and research have to be actively anti-sexist and antiracist; where 'non' is a passive, apolitical and often unconscious stance, 'anti' requires a conscious decision to engage actively with issues of racism and sexism at all levels of politics, from the personal to the international. As Elizabeth Spelman (1988: 4) says, 'If we think of privilege simply as appearing in individuals rather than being lodged in ways of thinking, we focus on what privilege feeds but not on what sustains it'. Development discourses sustain racialised and gendered privileges to the extent that they allow the charity model to stand in the place of analysis, assuming the goodness of people who would engage in development extends to their racism and sexism. It does not. One has only to consider this scenario during the one-week Inception Mission which followed CIDA's approval of our application. We all met for the first time, in Costa Rica. Private hotel rooms had been reserved for all the Canadians; shared rooms for the Nicaraguans and Hondurans.

The third point here is closely related to the previous two, and will form the basis for the remainder of the paper. There is a need, in development projects such as these, to examine what Foucault calls one's will to knowledge. Whether on a research trip, a teaching trip or a tourist trip, we who travel from the here of areas considered developed to the there of places considered not, need to account for the sense we make as we go, and our reasons for making it. We also need to examine the discourses into which will enter the stories we tell back home, for the currency we are hoping to trade in and what permits our access to such currency – what Valerie Walkerdine (1990) calls 'observations to which the observed have no access'. The work of feminist and post-colonial critics (eg Amos and Parmar, 1984; Fusco, 1995; Grewal and Kaplan, 1994; Jordan, 1989; Spivak, 1990, 1999; Trinh, 1989) have shown us that there is nothing at all pure about the 'pure curiosity' claimed to motivate so much mainstream/malestream research since the colonial period.

Anthropology, for example, was, according to Ruth Behar, 'born of the European colonial impulse to know others in order to lambaste them, better manage them, or exalt them' (1996: 4); others have offered similar descriptions of the history not only of anthropology but also of sociology and geography, at the very least (Apffel-Marglin and Sanchez, 2002; Mohanty, 1991; Phillips, 1995; Smith, 1999). While keeping ever mindful of these histories, I believe that it is possible to relocate our will-to-knowledge in friendship, with solidarity, and with witnessing.

Toward a Possible Methodology

In developing a methodology for the kind of work I do, I am arguing against two broad trends in research. The first, from the physical/natural sciences, is the idolisation of scientific method, the reliance on positivism, the desire for broad sweeping trends established by large numbers. As my Canadian soil science colleague said, 'why would you study one community when you could study a hundred'? Note that this was a methodological question, not one of adding 100 times more resources! Second, from the social sciences, is the claim that what researchers are doing is telling people who they are, whether the researcher is telling her research subjects or the rest of the world.

I have been informed by several cautionary notes, principally learned from feminist and anti-colonial researchers. We need an awareness of the power relations, of sex, class, race/ethnicity, age, region, religion, education level, or other axes of social inequality, and a recognition of the impossibility of operating outside these relations. There is a need for researchers to examine and name their own investments. And we need to work against the 'god-trick' of the myth of objectivity or view from nowhere (Haraway, 1988) which allows dominant views to be presented as universal and for context and history to be ignored. Further, these need to frame not only research relationships between people from so-called developed and developing nations, but also research relationships between variously-privileged people within nations, as well as the pedagogic relationships through which such methodologies might be taught.

It is possible that the cautions I have been making about research would lead one to the conclusion that it is better to do nothing at all. And indeed, students and others have found such constraints and prerequisites immobilising (Nagar, 2002). First, if we can never get outside power, and power is always seen in the liberal sense of power-over, an oppression from which we must free ourselves, then the researcher must simply retire and go home. Similarly, identity politics posits the idea that the only person who can know about a group of people is someone who is themselves a member of that group.

Yet this confuses ontology and epistemology, and results in the kind of scenario I endured many times while teaching social inequality. The only black student in the room would claim that they had never experienced racism, therefore there was no such thing, and the other, white, students in the class, glad to be freed from the responsibility of acknowledging the ways they perpetuate racism, would assume that the lone student of colour knew more about racism than I.

A second kind of immobilisation comes from the claim that, given the truth of the above, the only people who can be researched are those like oneself. There follows, where one is conscious, the recognition that, given the ongoing racially, ethnically, and sexually biased make-up of the population of funded researchers, this would mean an ongoing monopolisation of research about white, middle class, heterosexual people. And so, it may seem better to stop.

Lastly, the idea of social science research as being about telling people who they are, leads researchers to recognise that they have no business doing so, and so many stop. Sadly, those who continue are too often those who have no problem with the standard 'will to knowledge' excuses of dominant academe.

My own search has been for a methodology and ethics of research which acknowledges the problems mentioned above but does not find them immobilising, either for myself or for my students. And to find ways that these can be shared with researchers on both sides of the developed/developing divide.

And let me say that although we in academia are accustomed to making a distinction between our teaching and our research, research methods may in fact be the most pedagogic thing we do. Research methods are pedagogies, in the sense of Carmen Luke's (1996) *Peda-*

gogies of Everyday Life: they do not claim to teach, yet by their very existence they teach others where we think knowledge comes from, how we think it's produced, what we think it's important to know, who we think has or doesn't have knowledge, and how we think people should be treated in the process of creating it.

In this sense, methodologies are not simply actions or processes but statements of belief, of ethics – and not just what is narrowly called 'research ethics'. At least in the Research Ethics protocols in Canada, imperialism, sexism, racism and other exercises of unearned privileges and power are not precluded. On the contrary, any research which proposes to treat research subjects as equal participants, or proposes to take their perspective, or a radical perspective, or even proposes that there is such a thing as perspective in research, necessarily requires you to make a special case. The norm, the ethical violations these protocols are designed to stop are so blatant that the exercise of everyday forms of racism, sexism, classism, and imperialism, are invisible. If we want to engage in pedagogies which support social justice, we must find or create knowledge which is created through research methodologies which enact those beliefs.

Travelling Methodology?

However, if our southern colleagues are not using qualitative, feminist, anti-positivist, anti-imperialist methods, should we be trying to convince them to do so? Or is this just one more form of colonisation? I think there are reasons to offer up to 'third world' researchers a version of qualitative methods that, while still marginalised in terms of knowledge and truth, facilitates their making of knowledge in solidarity with marginalised peoples in their own societies in ways which do not reproduce the imperial gestures of dominant knowledge-making practices. Here I'm thinking both of the top-down gestures of much qualitative work as well as the exclusionary tendencies of positivist scholarship which privileges the visible and creates norms which disadvantage the different. This framing of top-down and positivist scholarship is itself the first reason for suggesting alternatives: as feminists have argued for several decades now, standard research methods have produced knowledge which oppresses rather than liberates women.

Such research methods, whether in the hands of local researchers, of sympathetic outsiders or of people who are consciously or unconsciously reproducing colonialist gestures, will not produce knowledge that will prove liberatory to marginalised peoples. They do produce knowledge of three types: knowledge useful to the career-building goals of Western academics; knowledge to satisfy the curiosity of those who think that curiosity is a sufficient basis for treating others as their 'Someone's private zoo', in Trinh's (1989: 82) all-too-accurate phrasing; and knowledge useful for the development project. How many women have how many children in how many poor communities? is a question the answer to which can justify any number of interventions in the name of development, particularly when we believe we already know the answer to the unasked question, why?

My experience also led me to think these would be useful methodologies. In my first involvement with URACCAN, I was asked to prepare some workshops on gender for the teaching staff. At that point, in 1997, URACCAN was a new university on the Caribbean coast of Nicaragua. The Atlantic Coast region of Nicaragua is an historically oppressed region, with all the tell-tale signs of a people marginalised by the dominant group, including being ethnically distinct from those in power, not having control over their abundant natural resources, and having low-quality schooling not in their first language.

During the Sandinista regime, a law was passed proclaiming the political, economic and cultural autonomy of the Atlantic Coast. Real autonomy, however, is never accomplished by decree, but by hard work and a relentless rebuilding of ways of thinking, acting, and organising life at all levels. A group of truly visionary people on the coast of Nicaragua were quick to say that autonomy would not be possible given the paucity of trained people, the legacy of centuries of bad education. So, they built a university, with the specific goals of training people who could manage both the natural and the human resources of the area, the latter to include finding ways to end the historic tensions between and hierarchies among the six ethnic groups.

In thinking about what I would do in these gender workshops, I was guided by my own images of what it meant that URACCAN was committed to anti-oppression struggles within regions in Nicaragua and in Latin America more broadly, and between racial and gender groups within the coastal region. My own intellectual commitments tied anti-oppression struggles to the struggle to unseat positivism as the singular method in the production and dispersal of knowledge. I was convinced, as I sat in the frozen north and planned my workshops, that the docentes (URACCAN's terms for its teaching staff) who would participate in my workshops would already be familiar with anti-positivist critiques. At the very least, I knew, they would welcome them.

To my surprise, neither was the case. The *docentes* generally seemed to me not to want to critique their own epistemological commitments, and instead to want facts which fitted their current frames. There are all kinds of potential explanations for the lack of acceptance of anti-positivist thought and methods, including the possibility that I presented them badly, due to poor pedagogy, inadequate Spanish skills and/or simple lack of time. It may also be true that, while studying gender requires at least the beginnings of a critique of positivism, in the sense that we have to see knowledge and society as constructed rather than found, it may well be that it is a poor starting point for exposure to anti-positivist thought, since the topic of gender seems to invoke so much resistance whenever and wherever it is discussed.

Although apparently contradictory, a second experience which contributed to my faith that these methods would be useful in the Central American context was that by the year 2000, when I taught research methods as part of the above-mentioned graduate programme at URACCAN, the resistance was already beginning to change. The Master's candidates were much more quickly able to see the internal colonialism of their own research projects; a shift in one proposal from what's wrong with the *Miskitu* students at URACCAN? to how is racism perpetuated at URACCAN? can serve as an example. Politically, the teaching faculty at URACCAN were committed to liberatory practices; in terms of research methods, though, they were unaware of how to put those commitments into practice. Once presented with alternative epistemologies and methodologies, however, projects moved along much more quickly and productively.

Lastly, research I conducted in my small, rural community in Canada demonstrated a similar problem with the epistemic privilege of (natural) science reinforcing the oppression of rural people, often at the hands of 'local colonialists' (Halperin, 1998; see also Heald, 2008). The similarities in the attitudes and approaches of community development experts at home and international development experts abroad led me to want to pursue the commonalities, and to a new commitment to debunking the privileges which enabled these kinds of paternalistic attitudes and approaches.

I argue, then, that one of the justifications for bringing knowledge of feminist, anti-colonial and anti-positivist methodologies and episte-mologies from the 'north' to the 'south' is because colonial education so privileged positivist, Western science, and so hid its social and poli-tical agendas and investments, that their adoption in 'native' research appears necessary and inevitable. The epistemic privilege of dominant forms of natural science, in which questions of epistemology, politics and oppression have been mooted, is thus perpetuated and reinforced by research which appears to be indigenous.

It may seem curious that my proposals for incorporating 'Qualitative Methodologies for Investigating Community Knowledge, Power and Gender' were much more readily accepted by my Nicaraguan and Honduran agronomist colleagues than by the Canadians. This, I would argue, gives credence to my claim not only that colonial re-search and pedagogic practices have temporarily foreclosed alter-natives, but also that development and the positivism of science are mutually supporting. A challenge to the methodologies and peda-gogies of scientists trained in the North is implicitly a challenge to the forms of superiority which allow knowledge transfer to be seen as unidirectional and helping to be seen as a good, and therefore in-contestable, endeavour which affirms the goodness of the people so involved.

All this said, I want to close by summarising a few seemingly mini-scule ways that I have worked towards such methodologies, whether researching or teaching qualitative methods for investigating power, gender and community, at home or abroad.

Conclusion

The first and constant task is to unsettle epistemologies. This involves engagement with debates concerning the received versus constructed view of knowledge; the myth of objectivity versus the 'elaborate specificity and loving care needed to see faithfully from another's point of view' (Haraway, 1988); situated knowledges versus a god's eye view or view from nowhere; and recognising the imperialism implicit in the separation between science and myth. Related to this, local knowledges have to be recognised and respected; this means giving up the dream of explaining everything and accepting, even welcoming and inviting, incommensurability (Schutte, 2000). According to Ellen and Harris (2000): 'The inherent ethnocentrism and elitism of late twentieth-century global science ... has made it difficult for scientists themselves to accept that the folk have any knowledge of worth ... a culture of denial which has been justified by a methodological reductionism and evaluative process which systematically renders such knowledge 'unscientific'. Scholars from the margins are needed to correct this 'culture of denial''.

Secondly, we might see the purpose of research as being not to learn about but to learn from people. This is related to Ruth Behar's (1996) notion of a 'vulnerable observer'. Vulnerability in research is not just about putting in personal information or expressing emotion. To be vulnerable is to confess to the people about whom you've been making sense just what you've been doing. To be vulnerable is to be accountable, and to try to find ways that the things you have to say can be heard, not to just escape into politeness. Being vulnerable is not about standing outside as the observer or the researcher or the teacher but taking the risk of having your interpretations rejected by those about whom you speak, all the while trying as hard as you can to say things in such a way that they won't be rejected. Reflexivity is about taking the risk of honesty. While many years of schooling have taught us *all* that being right is the most important thing, the notion of vulnerability asks us to consider how that need to be right is tied to the need for power, and what it would mean to give that up.

In a further, related, move, I try to see people as neither subjects nor objects of my research, nor necessarily collaborators or participants, but as friends. In this sense, I don't research up or down but face to face (Behar, 1996). I take this to mean not only that people are my equals, but that I also care about them, I care what I think of them and assume they care about that too. I try neither to glorify nor exalt them nor to lambaste and manage them, but to engage in a project aimed at mutual benefit.

But, in terms of the project with the Central American agronomists, this is all moot now. In the end, it was not the dynamics of race or gender that proved most salient, but the dominance of science. Indeed, it appeared, even knowledge of 'development' was unnecessary; if one knew about science, one could do 'development'. Hence the project director's claim that the only skill which would be needed by the project coordinator was knowledge of how to run a pesticide-fate model on the computer.

My own involvement in the project was sought because CIDA had mandated the inclusion of gender, but this apparently did not mean-to CIDA or to the project team-that a shift in what counted as know-ledge and who counted as knowledge-producers would be required. I was welcome to add gender, and even to add community, as long as such additions did not touch the core of what was to be done. The soil scientists have been able to believe in the inevitability of their 'facts', to exempt themselves from engaging in reflexivity about the power/knowledge relations in which they engage, and to leave unexamined the consequences of the epistemic privilege from which they benefit. Similarly, they were able to believe that they themselves were exempt from the dynamics that the community-based, critical research methods I was proposing would reveal. They were, apparently, able to believe that being nice, buying beer and smiling over it while unable to communicate, because no commonalities of language or experience had been established, was sufficient.

They were, it seems, able to accept that sufficient consultation had taken place with the so-called partners if said partners had been asked to provide a list of laboratory equipment or short courses they would like. There was no context – no knowledge that context even mattered – for knowing that the privilege of ever having been in a well equipped lab was not universally available. The very power dynamics which granted the Western scientists epistemic privilege left them unable to recognise or critique that privilege.

This failure to contextualise also extended to the very notion of development itself, so that while it appears evident to many that 'in-digenous environmental knowledge ... can hardly be ignored in development contexts and that it is an essential ingredient in any pragmatic development strategy, especially those which claim to achieve a degree of sustainability' (Ellen and Harris, 2000), such awareness was apparently unavailable and unnecessary in the conceptualisation and funding of this project. Instead, a straightforward north-south knowledge transfer was envisioned. In the context of our project, then, I can only imagine how unscientific must have appeared methods designed to elicit such knowledge.

But, while Ellen and Harris (2000) say that there has been a reversal of the practices of ignoring indigenous knowledge over the past 40 years, in this case, and in CIDA more broadly, ignorance of this trend is acceptable. This may partly be because of a kind of add-and-stir approach, where indigenous knowledge, like gender, can be added only to the extent that they do not threaten or demand change from dominant science. Where my knowledge let me see issues of racism, imperialism and paternalism at every turn, the scientists' knowledge, and its impact on their beliefs and behaviours, remained invisible.

Although I had spent considerable energy over two and a half years in the development of this project, I left. The immutability of the epistemic privilege that was to be afforded science, and the consequent impossibility of seeing the contradictions that this presented, could not be overcome.

While others may have been more willing or able to tolerate the contradictions, I am arguing that a failure to take seriously the ways science marginalises other epistemologies (not just indigenous ones but also feminist, anti-colonial and antiracist epistemologies), negates any effort to attend to gender, race, nation, class and educational inequalities. CIDA and the projects it funds can proceed as if feminist, post-colonial and post-development critiques had never happened, as if the racism, sexism and epistemological imperialism I experienced are inevitable consequences of development, just as they are of the education offered up as development.

As Seidman (1997: 48) has proposed, 'Once the veil of epistemic privilege is torn away, science appears as a social force enmeshed in particular cultural and institutional power struggles. The claim to truth, as Foucault has proposed, is inextricably an act of power'. What remains unclear for me is precisely how to tear away this veil. Methodologies meant to unseat power and privilege appear irrelevant to those whose privilege and power are unacknowledged precisely because of their privilege and power. Left to the rest of us is the consolation that more and more scholarship is able to go on in the margins and that more people are finding ways to speak truth to power. Left to us, too, apparently, is the continual questioning of our methodologies, our truths, and to whom and under what conditions it is acceptable to offer them.

Among the four basic attitudes Karen McCarthy Brown recommends we adopt is to 'hold truths lightly' (in Schaab, 2001). I agree, but at the same time it is apparently necessary to hold on tight in the face of those who would consider using their truths to perpetuate the very oppressions against which many of us try to work.

References

Amos, V and Parmar, P (1984) Challenging imperial feminism. *Feminist Review* 17(July) p3-19

Apffel-Marglin, F and Sanchez, L (2002) Developmentalist feminism and neocolonialism in Andean communities. In K Saunders (ed) *Feminist Post-Development Thought: rethinking modernity, post-colonialism and representation*. London: Zed Books

Behar, R. (1996) *The Vulnerable Observer: anthropology that breaks your heart*. Boston: Beacon Press

Luke, C. (1996) (ed) *Feminisms and pedagogies of everyday life*. Albany, NY: State University of New York Press.

Ellen, R and Harris, H (2000) Introduction. In R Ellen, P Parkes and A Bicker (eds) *Indigenous Environmental Knowledge and Its Transformations: critical anthropological perspectives*. Amsterdam: Harwood

Fusco, C (1995) *English is Broken Here: notes on cultural fusion in the Americas*. New York: The New Press

Grewal, I and Kaplan, C (eds) (1994) *Scattered Hegemonies: postmodernity and transnational feminist practices*. Minneapolis: University of Minnesota Press

Halperin, R (1998) *Practicing Community: class culture and power in an urban neighborhood*. Austin: University of Texas Press

Haraway, D (1988) Situated knowledges: the science question in feminism and the privilege of partial perspective. *Feminist Studies* 14(3) p575-599

Heald, S. (2008) Embracing Marginality: Place-making vs Development in Gardenton, Manitoba. *Development in Practice* 18(1) p 17-29

Jordan, J (1989) *Moving Towards Home: political essays*. London: Virago

Luke, C (ed) (1996) *Feminisms and Pedagogies of Everyday Life*. Albany: State University of New York

Mohanty, C (1991) Under western eyes: feminist scholarship and colonial discourses. In C Mohanty, A Russo and L Torres (eds) *Third World Women and the Politics of Feminism*. Bloomington: Indiana University Press.

Nagar, R (2002) Footloose researchers, 'travelling' theories, and the politics of transnational feminist praxis. *Gender, Place and Culture*, 9(2) 1p79-186

Phillips, L (1995) Difference, indifference and making a difference: reflexivity in the time of cholera. In S Cole and L Phillips (eds) *Ethnographic Feminisms: essays in anthropology*. Ottawa: Carleton University Press

Schaab, G (2001) Feminist theological methodology: toward a kaleidoscopic model. *Theological Studies* 62(2) p341-365

Schutte, O (2000) Cultural alterity: cross-cultural communication and feminist theory in north-south contexts. In U Narayan and S Harding (eds) *Decentering the Center: philosophy for a multicultural, postcolonial, and feminist world*. Bloomington: Indiana University Press

Seidman, S (1997) *Difference Troubles: queering social theory and sexual politics*. London: Cambridge Cultural Social Studies

Smith, L (1999) *Decolonizing Methodologies: research and indigenous peoples*. London: Zed Books

Spelman, E (1988) *Inessential Woman: problems of exclusion in feminist thought*. Boston: Beacon

Spivak, G (1990) *The Post-Colonial Critic: interviews, strategies, dialogues*. Sarah Harasym (ed) London: Routledge

Spivak, G (1999) *A Critique of Post-Colonial Reason: toward a history of the vanishing present*. Cambridge: Harvard University Press

Trinh, T (1989) *Woman, Native, Other: writing postcoloniality and feminism*. Bloomington: Indiana University Press

Walkerdine, V (1990) *Schoolgirl Fictions*. London: Verso

6

'A Better place to Live': School history textbooks, nationalist fantasies, and the incarcerating banality of white supremacy

KEN MONTGOMERY

The truths of white supremacy do not exist merely in the false taxonomies that humiliate and degrade, in profiled populations whose lives and movements are put under constant surveillance, in the minds of children tormented by racist name-calling, in whole populations of impoverished people devastated by globalisation, warfare and health epidemics, in racialised bodies that are punished, tortured, or hanged from tree limbs, nor in the skeletal mass remains of unspeakable genocides. Nor do the truths of white supremacy reside merely in anomalous and radically evil places, spaces, nations, or individuals. White supremacy also empowers, bestows unfair advantage, and procures privilege and benefits and, thus, the truths of white supremacy exist simultaneously in the minds, bodies, cultures, occupations, homes, vacations and bank accounts of racialised whites and in the most ordinary spaces, places and peoples (eg school textbooks).

In racial states such as Canada, 'white governance' prevails to the extent that policies and practices of multiculturalism have the effect not of disrupting white domination, but rather of making such domination appear invisible via representing it as given, normal, or commonsensical (Goldberg, 2002; Omi and Winant, 1994: 77-91). Disturbing, dismantling, or otherwise contesting such oppressive power thus necessitates a de-construction of the normalised and naturalised structures that sustain both racisms and the racial state itself. It is, in other words, about taking seriously the discursive powers that construct knowledge, police it, and put it into the world as normal or as just the way things are.

This chapter considers how racism permeates the taken-for-granted structures of schooling via some of the most commonplace and seemingly benign discursive practices and formations that give rise to 'regimes of truth' about the subject of Canada (Foucault, 1980). It is based on an analysis of the most recent Canadian history textbooks sanctioned for use in Ontario high schools by that province's Ministry of Education. An endless procession of multicultural policies, legislation, formal evaluative procedures, and Ministry of Education directives for authors and publishers, have been designed to ensure that school learning resources are more inclusive of diverse perspectives and experiences and free from bias, prejudice, racism, and other forms of discrimination (Gidney, 1999: 150-152).

While the representation of minoritised and marginalised groups in Canadian history textbooks has changed for the better as a result of such well-intentioned procedures and while overt racisms are obviously less of a problem now than they once were, I take issue with assumptions that either the textbooks or the nation whose history they narrate have become non- or even antiracist in their essence. I contend that these textbooks depict Canada as a space of antiracist achievement in a way that obscures the always present entanglements between racism and antiracism and those between race and state formation.

A dangerous complacency is thus permitted with respect to racisms by perpetuating myths about the essential tolerance of Canada and the dearth of racisms within it. There are white-robed and easily-identifiable racisms and then there are those racisms banally reproduced and less easy to perceive because they take the shape of unquestionably valid truths (Foucault, 1980; Green and Grosvenor, 1997: 884). It is the latter which are the focus of this chapter.

I am using Canadian history textbooks in this analysis as a cultural site to illustrate the embeddedness of racism within the banal structures and taken-for-granted experiences that organise life in a modern racial state. Specifically, this analysis considers how the ordering of conceptual knowledge about racism effectively flags the nation and reproduces an 'imagined community' of nationhood that, while perhaps not obvious or blatantly racist, is nonetheless white supremacist insofar as it supports the political and cultural empowerment of racialised whites (Anderson, 1991; Billig, 1995; Wetherell and Potter, 1992).

Speaking the truth about power in schools and nations

Although the nation is often taken for granted as some neutral entity, it does, in fact, articulate complexly in its boundary-making processes with constructs such as gender, race, sexuality, class, and colour to constitute subjectivities within interlocking systems of domination reproduced through such articulations (Alexander and Mohanty, 1997; Anthias and Yuval-Davis, 1992). Focusing on the connections between race, nation, and gender, for example, a number of scholars of feminist, antiracist, and postcolonial theory have documented how representations of the Canadian nation contribute to the marginalisation of women and racialised groups by painting a normalised image of the nation that is predominantly white and male (Bannerji, 2000; Dua and Robertson, 1999; Henry and Tator, 2002; Mackey, 2002; Razack, 2002; Strong-Boag, *et al.*, 1998). In the context of current world events in which the policing of nationalities and national boundaries has become so forceful and pervasive, and in which debates about the reasonable accommodation of racialised and religious minorities have come to preoccupy national politics across the globe, there would seem to be an imperative to understand more fully the multidimensional constructed-ness of these nations and their boundaries and, as well, the oppressive consequences of such constructions.

Schools have always had an explicit role to play in solidifying the symbolic boundaries of nation. School history textbooks, moreover, have traditionally been integral to instilling in the young a sense of unity, pride, and patriotism toward the nation. However, such seemingly benign apparatuses of the State (ie officially sanctioned history textbooks) are also violent in their effects insofar as they disseminate and legitimise hegemonic knowledge about racism as that which is done exclusively by evil, irrational, or ignorant people in distant nations and times (thus denying normalised or everyday racism), or else they reproduce fantasies of a particular nation as an antiracist exemplar for the world (thus denying the pervasiveness of racism within said nation or effective antiracisms elsewhere). I want to insist that racism be understood not as merely radical evil or obvious discrimination, but rather as banal, everyday experiences of racialised social oppressions that are discursively mediated and tied to the material world through social and political institutions of exclusionary/inclusionary power and through the consequences resulting from the defence and reproduction of this power. The benefit of such a conceptualisation is that it makes visible ways in which the state-sanctioned education system is clearly implicated in the production and reproduction of racisms in society (Dei, 1996; Stanley, 1995, 1998).

The cultures of schooling, childhood, and adolescence are racialised in ways that provide children and adolescents with meaningful ways to both understand and act in daily life (Hatcher and Troyna, 1993; Lewis, 2003; Troyna and Hatcher, 1992). This is not to suggest that racisms determine absolutely these understandings and actions, but rather that the grammars of racism steer children and youth toward particular hegemonic interpretations of difference and inequality (Rizvi, 1993). These grammars steer many, especially racialised whites, toward imprisoning dependencies upon meritocracy, individualism, and egalitarianism, which together, among other things, enable denials of racism, the negation of white capital, the repositioning of whites as victims of racism, an obfuscation of the processes and histories of appropriation that lead to white dominance, and colour-blind approaches to addressing social inequality (Gillborn, 2006; Leonardo, 2004; Rezai-Rashti, 2005; Solomon *et al*, 2005). In what follows, I illustrate how such grammars of racism articulate with the imagined community of nation, and especially via nationalist discourses of multicultural destiny and antiracist maturation, achievement, and redemption.

'A Better Place to Live'

The current Ontario Grade 10 History Curriculum outlines four specific expectations as part of an overall goal that students should be able, by the end of the course, to 'demonstrate an understanding of the elements of Canadian identity' (Province of Ontario: Ministry of Education, 1999: 28). Students are expected to learn how to explain the extent to which certain symbols represent Canada and Canadians, to evaluate the contributions to Canadian society of its communities, to demonstrate how artistic expression reflects Canadian identity, and to articulate why the Canadian government promotes a common Canadian identity through its various agencies. This explicit curricular stress on Canadian identity is reflected in the new crop of textbooks as well, which parade Canada's diverse ethnic composition as having given rise to a distinctive Canadian identity and suggesting that the promotion of such a common multicultural identity is the key to a tranquil and harmonious nation-state free of racisms (Bain *et al.*, 2000: 1; Bolotta, *et al.*, 2000: ix; Newman, 2000: 12). Each of the textbooks asserts that a unique Canadian identity and culture exists (despite the apparent threat posed by the influence of American culture) and each repeats the idea that Canada is one of the best countries in the world in which to live, often citing UN rankings placing Canada at the top of its Human Development Index to support the claim (eg Bolotta *et al.*, 2000: 331; Fielding and Evans, 2000: 338). *Canadian History*, for example, reads:

> Living in Canada today we are not free of worries and concerns. We have political and constitutional problems regarding power-sharing between levels of government. We have problems with the equitable sharing of wealth and with outside influences on our economy. We have incidents of discrimination and intolerance despite guarantees to our rights. Yet Statistics Canada surveys show that most Canadians feel a physical sense of well-being, and most would agree with the UN that Canada is the best place in the world to live. (Hundey et al., 2000: 438)

This passage boasting of Canada's place in the world reduces all forms of social oppression (including racism) to episodic instances of intolerance. Such negation of the structural and historical persistence of racism is a discursive pattern to be found inside school systems and beyond and one commonly enacted by racialised whites in positions of power and authority (Henry and Tator, 2002; Varma-Joshi *et al.*,

2004). I have elsewhere made the argument that these same textbooks consistently reduce racism to irrational, abnormal, extreme, and individualised problems of psychological or moral deficit. They are represented as either foreign to Canada, isolated incidents within Canada, or part of a distant past and with consequences solely for the racially subjugated (Montgomery, 2005b). Here I am concerned with how this reductive conception of racism articulates with the redundant marking of Canada as a better place to live.

What makes Canada so wonderful, according to these textbooks, is the multicultural aspect of its identity, which supposedly permits tolerance of difference. Canada is made of many peoples with different heritages happily sharing in the shaping of Canadian society. As put in *Canada: Face of a Nation*:

> Canada has a multicultural society where people from different cultures are encouraged to preserve their original languages, their religions, and many of their beliefs and customs, as they join and contribute to Canadian society ... interaction among these groups also creates more tolerance of differences and makes Canada *a better place to live*. (Bolotta *et al.*, 2000: x)

One can ask by what sort of institutionalised arrogance and structural self-congratulatory satisfaction does it become possible to claim (and to define as state-sanctioned high school knowledge) an entire nation-state to be a better place to live than any, or even most, others? The textbooks, even as they have come to document the violence enacted against multiple racialised groups within Canada, effectively erase such violence and its consequences with their proud assertions about Canada's superiority. Such obliterations are symbolically violent not only in what they eradicate from historical and contemporary spaces within Canada, but also in their egotistical vanquishing of lives, experiences, knowledges, and histories that exist beyond the geopolitical boundaries and historical timeline of Canada, and are surely better (ie less racist) than anything within Canada.

Who opposes racism?

I have argued elsewhere that these Canadian history textbooks reduce racism to individualised and isolated incidents that are largely contained to the past and that they permit an 18th century idea of race as natural or biological to subtly circulate, but that they do so even while paying a great deal of explicit attention to racism (Montgomery, 2005). Here I am asking how the textbooks represent opposition to this racism, which is given so much more narrative space than in previous generations. Who, in other words, opposes racism, for what purposes, and with what consequences?

Most of the textbooks which cite the role of the federal government in attempting to forcibly assimilate Native peoples, highlight the use of residential schools as an especially damaging component of this attempt at assimilation and, significantly, illustrate that Aboriginal peoples worked against the injustices that infringed upon their cultures, traditions, land and human rights (eg Bain *et al.*, 2000: 122; Bolotta *et al.*, 2000: 77). A select few male leaders (eg Mohawk Chief F.O. Lott) are represented as standing for the category of 'Aboriginal people' and heralded as initiating an 'Aboriginal activism that would blossom in the 1960s' (Newman, 2000: 187). Such representations obscure the unbroken line of activism (eg by both male and female Aboriginal persons) regarding their land rights by positioning these mid-twentieth century male Aboriginal activists as the founders of change. These representations also suggest that progressive transformation was inevitably on its way. Put differently, while the federal government's actions are clearly portrayed in a negative and oppressive light, they are also represented as somehow confined to an era in which the groundwork for improved relations between Aboriginal nations and the Canadian government was already being set.

The inevitability or destiny of such good relations is frequently illustrated through the insertion of the present into or alongside these narratives of the past. For example, a chronological narrative about Aboriginal political movements that arose in response to the forced assimilation policies of the Canadian government is broken in *Spotlight Canada* with a fast forward section of text declaring that 'In 1998, the Canadian government made a formal apology to Aboriginal peoples for the treatment they received in residential schools' (Cruxton and Wilson, 2000: 145).

Indeed, there is a recognisable pattern by which these textbooks discuss numerous racisms of the past, but frequently depict each as an incident resolved or eventually redressed, if only quite belatedly, through the actions of one state apparatus or another. Not only, therefore, is Canada imagined to be better than other places because of its apparently unique tolerance, but it is also depicted as being better than its older self. This redemptive and retroactively antiracist representation is perhaps best illustrated through what is consistently referred to as the most shameful incident of racism in Canadian history: the internment of Japanese Canadians during WWII.

Most of the textbooks conclude narrative sections dealing with the experiences of Japanese Canadians during World War II by tagging on a sentence or short paragraph indicating that the Canadian government apologised to Japanese Canadians for past injustices and offered financial compensation to individual survivors (Bolotta *et al.*, 2000: 172). One textbook, *Canadian History*, simply reprinted the government advertisement placed in newspapers to announce the redress settlement (Hundey *et al.*, 2000: 239). There is virtually no explanation about what was involved in getting the federal apology and financial compensation.

The lifetime of hard work carried out by Canadian citizens interned during the war and others who viewed this as an injustice in need of redress is entirely obscured along with the long history of successive politicians' reluctance and outright refusal to agree to such a redress settlement (Sunahara, 1981). Redress, in these narratives, functions to sustain the national imaginary of Canada as a just society and the Canadian state as one that would undo the racist injustice of the past by voluntarily making reparations in the present.

There are several references to organisations explicitly identified as having fought 'racial intolerance' (eg the Canadian Association for the Advancement of Coloured People) and which are deemed to have been politically active and successful in their efforts to lobby for 'improved civil rights' and 'antiracist legislation' (Cruxton and Wilson, 2000: 357; Hundey *et al.*, 2000: 235). However, the nation's moral reformation is discursively centred in these accounts, while the antiracist efforts of those people made objects of racialised exclusions are marginalised. The lack of details regarding the historical contributions of those involved in advancing the cause of civil rights and successfully bringing in legislation to combat racial discrimination suggest that such details are somehow less critical to the national story than the knowledge that Canada has made significant progress in extending human rights and, moreover, that it was destined to do so. In *Canadian History* it appears that the efforts of racialised minorities to combat racism are most useful insofar as they facilitate an illustration that Canada made significant progress in the realm of human rights and that, in fact, that some Canadian provinces were even ahead of their time in that regard.

> The wartime contributions of Blacks, Aboriginal peoples, and other minorities advanced the cause of civil rights after the war. By 1945, Ontario and Alberta had legislated against racial and religious discrimination in hiring and housing – the first provinces to do so. Over the second half of the century, the rights of Canadians were extended in provincial and federal human rights legislation. (Hundey *et al.*, 2000: 245)

The subject of Canada is similarly central with respect to depictions of prominent Black Canadians in the post-WWII period who are said to have actively opposed racism. For example, Carrie Best is described in several textbooks as a 'lifelong champion of human rights' who fought against 'racist laws' and who 'helped change antiracism strategies in Canada' (Bolotta *et al.*, 2000: 192; Fielding and Evans, 2000: 228-229). However, the narrative figure of Best is consistently prone to textual segregation, by being positioned in side-bars or so-called 'hidden story' boxes. Certainly Best's lifelong work was not hidden from those who read her paper *The Clarion* or from many Black Canadians. Is this knowledge of Best therefore hidden or ignored and if the latter, what are the implications of it being called the former? Given the stated significance of Best's work, the exclusion of her story from the main narrative suggests that her work is of more relevance to Black Canadians than it is to all residents of Canada and this, in turn, is indicative of a perception of racism which ignores the fact that privilege is accrued by some (eg racialised whites) even as others (eg racialised minorities) are subjected to the consequences of racism. Moreover, while Best's efforts are represented as impacting upon governments and 'antiracism strategies in Canada,' the 'only solution' (ie 'outlawing racial discrimination') is one made by the implied and ever present figure of Canada (Fielding and Evans, 2000: 228-229). In other words, Carrie Best, one of the few women of colour represented with much detail at all, functions in these narratives as a trope for the maturation into goodness and tolerance of the Canadian national body.

Certainly some acknowledgement is directed toward the efforts of Black Canadians like Rosemary Brown and Lincoln Alexander in lobbying for civil rights, but primarily it is state apparatuses like the Supreme Court and certain white male political leaders standing for the nation (eg Prime Ministers Diefenbaker and Trudeau) that are credited with championing human rights and racial equality, presumably making the country a better place to live (eg Bogle *et al.*, 2000: 345). Diefenbaker's Bill of Rights 'that rejected discrimination on the basis of race' and Trudeau's Charter of Rights and Freedoms designed 'to end racial discrimination within Canada' (Cruxton and Wilson, 2000: 309; Fielding and Evans, 2000: 290) are among the many references propping up an image of Canada as a nation actively transforming itself into a just, even antiracist, society. Opposition to racism (ie antiracism) is positioned in these textbooks as the normal condition practiced vigorously by 'many Canadians' who 'struggled to make Canada and the world a better place through the promotion of human rights' (Bolotta *et al.*, 2000: 342).

Consequently Canada is represented as a redeemed and just nation, a representation enhanced by persistent references to the spirit of tolerance deemed to characterise the Canadian identity. The 'riddle of Canadian identity' according to *Canada: A Nation Unfolding* 'lies in the relative harmony in which its citizens have come to live' and the manner by which 'Canadians from coast to coast' have constructed a tolerant and 'cosmopolitan society tolerant of cultural and religious differences' (Newman, 2000: 8). These textbooks frequently make clear that things have not always been harmonious in Canada's historical path toward its imagined multicultural destiny, but they also privilege the view that the present is predominantly a picture of multicultural bliss. The multicultural perfection of the present redeems the racism of the past in these textbooks since Canadians have, with few exceptions, presumably become energetic antiracists and Canada itself a place defined by its racial egalitarianism. It is not merely that the mosaic model has been accepted in Canada, nor that such a model has been effective in creating a just and tolerant nation no longer substantially troubled by racisms or other social oppressions. It is more than this. State multiculturalism is represented as having successfully configured opposition to racism as the essence of Canadian identity and this vigorous and ethical stance against racism is deemed fundamental to understanding both Canadian distinctiveness and the perceived dearth of racism in Canadian society.

In these recent textbooks, which make explicit the racisms of Canada's past and present and the various actions taken to overcome them, the idea of being against racism is clearly attached to the state itself while the antiracist struggles of oppressed groups and their allies are obscured or marginalised. That is to say, these texts make clear that Canada has been antiracist or at least instrumental in stopping racism. Opposition to a racism that is conceived as prejudice and discrimination is central to Canadian identity and is, moreover, deemed to have become an achieved reality of the current Canada through commitments to justice and tolerance brought about with official multiculturalism.

In the logic of these new textbooks, Canada is a better place to live precisely because of its supposed dearth of racism and corresponding wealth of antiracism (or minimally a nation-wide conviction to redress, repair, and refrain from racisms) and it is multiculturalism that ensures this. There is in these textbooks a forceful assertion that the essential and unifying trait of Canadian society must be defended by respecting and tolerating differences. This differentialist assertion is paradoxically juxtaposed with an assimilative goal of unifying everyone and all difference under the nationalist umbrella of Canadian identity (Day, 2000). Canadian society is defended (from racists and racisms, but also from that which fractures society – namely difference) by the illusion of multicultural destiny, which controls, limits, and manages difference in part by encapsulating it within a multicultural bubble of homogeneity deemed Canadian identity, which paradoxically depends upon the rhetoric of heterogeneity.

The Violent Illusion of Destiny

A common thread running through the various generations of state-sanctioned textbooks is that Canada is somehow better than elsewhere and better than it once was – in large part because it has fulfilled its presumed destiny of finding harmonious ways to tolerate racialised others. Canada is depicted as better in part because those few acknowledged racisms attributed to the space of Canada have been overcome through the formation of a tolerant multicultural nation. That is to say, multiculturalism is envisioned both as the essence of Canadian identity and as that which stops racism in its tracks.

Imagined as having matured to a perfected state of tolerance and multiculturalism, and imagined as having a long history rooted in multicultural beginnings and destined for multicultural greatness, Canada gets depicted both as a nation redeemed and as a model for other nations to emulate. This imagined representation of Canada of course hinges on a redemption of the nation that obscures, denies, forgets, and minimises the racism of past and present and the violence inherent to it, that is, those denials of humanity that take their toll in lives, life chances, and life fulfilments. Canada is redeemed by these depictions of it having done antiracism to make up for the bits of racism in its past, but also gloriously positioned as a better place to live in which state-sanctioned multiculturalism ensures that racism never becomes 'here', what it surely is, 'there'.

Despite the prevalence in recent years of antiracist educational research and theory that conceptualises racism as a pervasive and multi-faceted phenomena tied to the reproduction of exclusionary institutional power, even these most recent state-sanctioned textbooks continue to adhere to, and are dominated by, differentialist (ie colour-conscious) and universalist (ie colour-blind) orientations to opposing racism (Bonnett, 2000). That is, racisms are deemed to be best dealt with by recognising, tolerating, celebrating and even respecting certain differences, but only within a nationalist framework that assimilates these very differences (and excludes others) into a universalistic category of 'Canadian' under which all should be treated equally. There is a strong sense, too, that the textbooks conceive of racism as that which can be eliminated or stopped, in part because it is conceived as 'readily extricable from everything else', and most particularly extricable from the nation-state itself (Gilroy, 2002: 251).

In the history textbooks analysed in this chapter, the very promotion of Canada as a better place to live and, as a now racism-free or anti-racist space, obscures the Canadian state's complicity in the ongoing global conditions that sustain and reproduce white supremacy. If Canada is a better place it is only *because* it is a state that contributes to the exploitation of lands, resources, and peoples of other nations (including those which it has displaced from its own geographical location) and the perpetuation of suffering under global white governance. The promotion of Canada as a better place to live and as non-racist, antiracist, only formerly racist, or even as less racist, entails as well a planetary separation whereby Canada is imagined to be extricable from elsewhere. Its socially constructed, historically constituted, and rather arbitrarily designated geopolitical lines, are reified to support a mythological state conceived as a detached place of innocence or as a segregated zone of near pluralistic perfection, untainted by racist oppression and exploitation and destined to lead the rest of the planet to some tolerant utopia.

This normalised fantasy of nationalist multicultural destiny is the modern day equivalent of the 'white man's burden'. It is not, then, simply the white-hooded, white-robed, neo-Nazi version of white supremacy that is of concern, but another more insidious variant – indeed it is no variant at all – that takes the form of 'normal'.

The myths advanced by the textbooks (and by the state itself insofar as these are state authorised texts) pertaining to an imagined Canada that is a utopian place of antiracist goodness and moral betterment, are dangerous and spurious not only because they contain racisms to temporal moments of the past or present. But also obscure racisms, the experiences and knowledges of racialised objects, and the processes by which racialised dominance is secured. They also privilege in the future white supremacist racisms by representing and promoting the Canadian nation as one rooted in a morally-solid inheritance from Europe that has prepared (implicitly white) Canadians to do good things in the world for (implicitly inferior) Others (Montgomery, 2006; Razack, 2004). The consequences of such representations for student-readers racialised as non-white (eg disengagement, vocal or physical resistance, dropping-out) can and do contribute to power differentials that sustain white domination (Dei *et al.*, 1997; Raby, 2004; Varma-Joshi *et al.*, 2004).

I have argued that the circulation of this knowledge about racism helps to sustain or prop up particular nationalist mythologies, most notably the myth of Canada as a uniquely tolerant and pluralistic nation-state which has effectively reduced and contained, if not altogether eliminated, racism, making Canada a better place to live, a model for other nations to emulate, and a place with a moral responsibility to uplift apparently inferior places in the world (Montgomery, 2006). The essence of white racist privilege is precisely this sort of institutionalised arrogance which positions Canada in mandated text-books as a morally superior nation blessed with an abundance of goodness and therefore burdened with an obligation to assist or uplift Others and Other places. Despite the certainty that antiracisms have also organised, shaped, been represented by, reproduced through, and to various degrees even privileged within these recent history text-books, these cultural texts continue to reproduce representations of the nation and national belonging that structure taken-for-granted advantage and dominating power for people racialised as white. They do so behind incarcerating mythologies of multiculturalism, which makes it exceedingly difficult for the privileged and empowered to break free and comprehend the truth about the reproduction of im-balanced power relations. A term with the semantic virtue of clearly signalling reference to such institutionalised reproduction of power is 'white supremacy' (Mills, 1998).

References

Alexander, M and Mohanty, C (eds) (1997) *Feminist Genealogies, Colonial Legacies, Democratic Futures*. New York: Routledge

Anderson, B (1991) *Imagined Communities: reflections on the origin and spread of nationalism*. London: Verso.

Anthias, F and Yuval-Davis, N (1992) *Racialized Boundaries: race, nation, gender, colour and class and the anti-racist struggle*. London: Routledge

Bain, C, DesRivieres, D, Flaherty, P, Goodman, D, Schemenauer, E and Scully, A (2000) *Making History – The Story of Canada in the Twentieth Century*. Toronto: Pearson Education Canada

Bannerji, H (2000) *The Dark Side of the Nation: essays on multiculturalism, nationalism and gender*. Toronto: Canadian Scholars Press Inc

Billig, M (1995) *Banal Nationalism*. London: Sage

Bogle, D, D'Orazio, E, and Quinlan, D (2000) *Canada: continuity and change*. Markham, Ontario: Fitzhenry and Whiteside

Bolotta, A, Hawkes, C, Jarman, F, Keirstead, M and Watt, J (2000) *Canada: face of a nation*. Toronto: Gage Educational Publishing Company

Bonnett, A (2000) *Anti-racism*. London: Routledge

Cruxton, J and Wilson, W (2000) *Spotlight Canada, 4th edition*. Toronto: Oxford

Day, R (2000) *Multiculturalism and the History of Canadian Diversity*. Toronto: University of Toronto Press

Dei, G (1996) *Anti-racism Education: theory and practice*. Halifax, NS: Fernwood Publishing

Dei, G, Mazzuca, J, McIsaac, E and Zine, J (1997) *Reconstructing Drop-Out: a critical ethnography of the dynamics of black students' disengagement from school*. Toronto: University of Toronto Press

Dua, E and Robertson, A (eds) (1999) *Scratching the Surface: Canadian anti-racist feminist thought*. Toronto: Women's Press

Fielding, J and Evans, R (2000) *Canada: our century, our story*. Scarborough, Ontario: Nelson Thomas Learning

Foucault, M (1980) Truth and power (translated by C Gordon, L Marshall, J Mepham and K Soper). In C Gordon (ed), *Power/Knowledge: selected interviews and other writings 1972-1977*. New York: Pantheon Books

Gidney, R (1999) *From Hope to Harris: the reshaping of Ontario's schools*. Toronto: University of Toronto Press

Gillborn, D (2006) Rethinking white supremacy: who counts in 'WhiteWorld'. *Ethnicities* 6(3) p318-340

Gilroy, P (2002) The end of antiracism. In P Essed and D Goldberg (eds) *Race Critical Theories: text and context*. Malden, Ma: Blackwell Publishers

Goldberg, D (2002) *The Racial State*. Malden, Ma: Blackwell Publishers Inc

Green, M and Grosvenor, I (1997) Making subjects: history-writing, education and race categories. *Paedagogica Historica*, XXXIII(3) p883-908

Hatcher, R and Troyna, B (1993) Racialisation and children. In C McCarthy and W Crichlow (eds) *Race, Identity and Representation in Education*. New York: Routledge

Henry, F and Tator, C (2002) *Discourses of Domination: racial bias in the Canadian English-language press*. Toronto: University of Toronto Press

Hundey, I, Magarrey, M and Pettit, N (2000) *Canadian History: 1900-2000*. Toronto: Irwin Publishing

Leonardo, Z (2004) The color of supremacy: beyond the discourse of 'white privilege'. *Journal of Educational Philosophy and Theory* 36(2) p137-152

Lewis, A (2003) Everyday race-making: navigating racial boundaries in schools. *American Behavioural Scientist* 47(3) p283-305

Lewis, A (2004) 'What group?' Studying whites and whiteness in the era of 'color-blindness'. *Sociological Theory* 22(4) p623-646

Mackey, E (2002) *The House of Difference: cultural politics and national identity in Canada*. Toronto: University of Toronto Press

Mills, C (1998) *Blackness Visible: essays on philosophy and race*. London: Cornell University Press

Montgomery, K (2005a) Banal race-thinking: ties of blood, Canadian history textbooks, and ethnic nationalism. *Paedagogica Historica* 41(3) p315-338

Montgomery, K (2005b) Imagining the antiracist state: representations of racism in Canadian history textbooks. *Discourse: Studies in the Cultural Politics of Education* 26(4) p427-442

Montgomery, K (2006) Racialized hegemony and nationalist mythologies: representations of war and peace in high school history textbooks, 1945-2005. *Journal of Peace Education* 3(1) p19-38

Newman, G (2000) *Canada: a nation unfolding, Ontario edition*. Toronto: McGraw-Hill Ryerson Limited

Omi, M and Winant, H (1994) *Racial formation in the United States: from the 1960s to the 1990s, 2nd edition*. New York: Routledge

Province of Ontario: Ministry of Education (1999) *The Ontario Curriculum Grades 9 and 10: Canadian and World Studies*. Toronto: Queen's Printer for Ontario

Raby, R (2004) 'There's no racism at my school, it's just joking around': ramifications for anti-racist education. *Race Ethnicity and Education* 7(4) p367-383

Razack, S (2004) *Dark Threats and White Knights: the Somalia affair, peacekeeping, and the new imperialism*. Toronto: University of Toronto Press

Razack, S (ed) (2002) *Race, Space, and the Law: unmapping a white settler society*. Toronto: Between the Lines

Rezai-Rashti, G (2005) The persistence of colonial discourse: race, gender, and Muslim students in Canadian schools. In V Zawilski and C Levine-Rasky (eds) *Inequality in*

Canada: a reader on the intersections of gender, race, and class. Don Mills, Ontario: Oxford University Press

Rizvi, F (1993) Children and the grammar of popular racism. In C McCarthy and W Chrichlow (eds) *Race, Identity and Representation in Education.* New York: Routledge

Solomon, P, Portelli, J, Daniels, B-J and Campbella, A (2005) The discourse of denial: how white teacher candidates construct race, racism, and 'white privilege'. *Race, Ethnicity and Education* 8(2) p147-169

Stanley, T (1995) White supremacy and the rhetoric of educational indoctrination: a Canadian case study. In J Barman (ed) *Children, Teachers, and Schools in the History of British Columbia.* Calgary: Detselig Enterprises

Stanley, T (1998) The struggle for history: historical narratives and anti-racist pedagogy. *Discourse: Studies in the Cultural Politics of Education* 19(1) p41-52

Strong-Boag, V, Grace, S, Eisenberg, A and Anderson, J (eds) (1998) *Painting the Maple: essays on race, gender, and the construction of Canada.* Vancouver: University of British Columbia Press

Sunahara, A (1981) *The Politics of Racism: the uprooting of Japanese Canadians during the Second World War.* Toronto: James Lorimer and Company Publishers

Troyna, B and Hatcher, R (1992) *Racism in Children's Lives: A study of mainly-white primary schools.* London: Routledge

Varma-Joshi, M, Baker, C and Tanaka, C (2004) Names will never hurt me? *Harvard Educational Review* 74(2) p175-208

Wetherell, M and Potter, J (1992) *Mapping the Language of Racism: discourse and the legitimation of exploitation.* New York: Harvestor Wheatsheaf

7

Narrative Research, Narrative Capital, Narrative Capability

MICHAEL WATTS

Life history research resonates with issues of discourse, power and resistance. By filling in the spaces between statistical numbers with the lived experiences of those who have been disempowered by hegemonic discourses, life history has the potential to be an ideal methodology of resistance. This chapter sets out to consider its potential. Drawing on Bourdieu's concepts of social and cultural capital, and illustrated by examples from a series of recent life history projects, it considers the narrative capital of research participants – the power they have to tell the stories of their lives. This narrative capital is then located in the field of educational research and Sen's capability approach is introduced to prompt the question: what real opportunities do research participants have to tell the stories they value and have reason to value? It is argued that narrative capital can be too easily squandered by the failure to recognise individual values. The chapter concludes with a call to open up the spaces that allow narrative research to generate this capital, giving the disempowered the substantive freedoms (or capability) to resist powerful hegemonies.

There are many forms of narrative research (Bruner, 1986; Polkinghorne, 1995; Lieblich *et al.*, 1998; Miller, 2000; Roberts, 2002) and the distinction between them is not always clear. Here I want to focus on life history research and, in particular, the influence of narrative capital (the power to tell stories) and narrative capability (the freedom to do so) on the shift from life stories to life histories (Goodson and Walker, 1991; Goodson and Sikes, 2001). Telling stories helps people make sense of their lives. Locating the stories they tell in wider social and political contexts helps us to understand the deeper social constructions that shape their lives. As Goodson and Sikes explain, 'without contextual commentary on issues of time and space, life stories remain uncoupled from the conditions of their social construction. This, above all, is the argument for life histories rather than life stories' (2001: 17). Capital and capability are both social constructions and, therefore, condition the telling of the life story and its transformation into life history.

Narrative Capital

Bourdieu conceptualises capital as resources and commodities that become objects of struggle because of their value in social relations of power: they are the stake in the 'competition for a power that can only be won from others competing for the same power' (Bourdieu, 2000: 241). He identifies four main types of capital (Bourdieu, 1991: 229-31): economic capital, social capital, cultural capital and symbolic capital.

Economic capital is monetary wealth that has been inherited or generated through economic activity. Social capital embraces the various kinds of valued and important relationships with others (such as networks, connections and group membership) that generate social processes and are deployed in pursuit of favour and advancement. Cultural capital exists in three forms: in an embodied state (eg in long-lasting dispositions of the mind and body that sensitise the individual to cultural distinctions), in an objectified state in the form of cultural goods (particularly those associated with 'high culture' such as books, works of art, etc) and in an institutionalised state (where it includes such things as educational qualifications). Symbolic capital includes prestige and social honour as well as personal qualities such as authority and charisma but is also the form that other types of capital assume once they are perceived and recognised as legitimate.

Other forms of capital include academic and educational capital (Bourdieu, 1988, 1993, 1996), emotional capital (Reay, 2000; Gillies, 2006), juridical capital (Bourdieu, 1998), linguistic capital (Bourdieu,

1991), physical capital (Shilling, 2004) and political and professional capital (Bourdieu, 1991, 1998).

In theorising this concept of capital, Bourdieu is simultaneously seeking to extend the notion of capital beyond its most visible and basic economic characteristics and acknowledging that each form of capital 'requires and is the product of an investment of an appropriate kind [which] can secure a return to that investment' (Moore, 2004: 446). The power of capital is to be found not simply in its accumulation but in its appropriate and strategic deployment. Bourdieu turns to the metaphor of the gaming table to illustrate this (1993: 34) and, drawing on the work of Reay (2000), Gillies suggests that parental involvement must return a profit for the child to be considered as emotional capital (2006: 284). Thus, with the economic metaphor running through them, these forms of capital, even when they are overlaid with other values such as the aesthetics of cultural capital, serve a mercantile purpose in the exchange of social relations. Capital, in this Bourdieusian sense, is the transmutation (1993: 32-33) or transubstantiation (Moore, 2004) of the interests of dominant interest groups and satisfies the instrumental aim of producing and reproducing social hierarchies and establishing the individual's place within them.

But what of narrative capital? Given that linguistic capital and the linguistic components of cultural capital have already been comprehensively addressed, is there a place for this particular form of storytelling capital? The simple answer (at least from this Bourdieusian perspective) is: Yes. Capital achieves its most effective instrumental purpose when it is deployed in the appropriate field. However, to construct the field 'one must identify the forms of specific capital that operate within it, and to construct the forms of specific capital one must know the specific logic of the field' (Bourdieu and Wacquant, 1992: 108). It thus seems appropriate that if life history participants are to be invited into the field of educational research, or social science research more generally, we should have a clearer understanding of the particular form of capital that defines and operates within it and how that capital is produced, accumulated, reproduced and – for those with less of it – kept in its place. In this context of confronting power, then, narrative capital seems all the more pertinent if our concern is to provide the otherwise disadvantaged with the capital required to articulate the stories of their lives.

So what constitutes narrative capital? It is more than simply having a good story to tell – although, given the interchangeability of capital, this can be discerned in, for example, 'dining out on a good story' (or, conversely, the absence of free lunches) and in the increasing popularity of celebrity autobiographies. The presumption here is that everyone has a story to tell but the different lives and lifestyles that frame the stories we tell of ourselves are valued differently. However, there are two interrelated aspects here: the value of the story and the way it is told.

I want to locate these two aspects of narrative capital in the particular sub-field of research on widening participation in higher education and to compare the participants in three narrative research projects undertaken in the UK: the experiences of state school students entering the elite Universities of Oxford and Cambridge (Watts, 2002, 2007), the aspirations and achievements of young people not progressing beyond compulsory education (Watts and Bridges, 2004, 2006) and the educational needs of refugees (Watts and Bridges, 2005; Watts, 2007b). Even these briefest of descriptions indicate the relative positions within the sub-field of the participants in these studies: the first group typically had much greater reserves of cultural capital – the main educational currency – than the latter two.

The narrative capital feeding the stories these participants told could almost be measured in the length of time it took to tell them. With detailed descriptions of school, college, extra curricular activities and their educational value, progression to post-compulsory education, deciding on universities, considering the extra investments that may have been necessary to give them a chance of getting in, and reflecting on the whole lot, the Oxbridge students had lengthy stories to tell. Once they had described their disaffection and their desire to leave at the first opportunity, the young people who had left school typically began running out of things to say and without the encouragement to continue and to reflect upon why they had not fitted in, why the teachers had not supported them and so on, few of them would have said much more. The refugees had deeply moving stories to tell but some of these stories were rendered much shorter than they should have been because they did not have the necessary language skills to tell them.

This, then, leads into the second aspect of narrative capital: the articulation of the story being told. Within education systems it is typically assumed that students have the required 'linguistic and cultural capital – and the capacity to invest it profitably – which the system presupposes and consecrates without ever expressly demanding it and without methodically transmitting it' (Bourdieu and Passeron, 1977: 99). This linguistic power can be subject to negotiation but 'it goes without saying that the capacity to manipulate is greater the more capital one possesses' (Bourdieu, 1991: 71). In these studies, the narrative capital of the participants can be seen as the transubstantiation of these other capitals.

The Oxbridge students typically had more stories to tell about their educational experiences and more ability to tell them. The young people who had left school had other stories to tell, stories that had little to do with formal education and that were written in the margins of their school lives, and they typically did not have the full range of linguistic skills to tell them. Some of the refugees were even more hampered by their lack of command of English: they told the stories of their lives competently but without the rhetorical flourishes and tricks available to native speakers.

Put another way, the more capital possessed by the participants, the greater their capacity to manipulate the stories they were telling: whereas the Oxbridge students were taking their stories out of brightly coloured crepe fastened with bows and ribbons, the young people having left school and the refugees were unwrapping them from functional brown paper sometimes done up with string.

However, if the greater linguistic skills of those research participants with greater volumes of capital made for more enchanting and enticing stories, stories that were more believable for no other reason than that they were well told, there is another and more insidious form of capital lurking behind the narrative capital of some of these participants: the symbolic capital that is the form other types of capital assume once they are perceived and recognised as legitimate.

Symbolic Capital: Telling Good Stories

This additional value accruing to the socially sanctioned possession of other forms of capital is how the rich become richer while the poor become poorer:

> One of the most unequal of all distributions, and probably, in any case, the most cruel, is the distribution of symbolic capital, that is, of social importance and of reasons for living ... there is no worse dispossession, no worse privation, perhaps, than that of the losers in the symbolic struggle for recognition, for access to a socially recognised social being, in a word, to humanity. (Bourdieu, 2000: 241)

Symbolic capital can significantly influence the telling of a tale because the narrative field must necessarily overlap with the field that is the focus of the tale. When researching higher education it is therefore inevitable that we will step into the field of education where manifestations of cultural capital are salient. Those research participants possessing greater volumes of cultural capital are more likely to recognise themselves as legitimate participants in that field and so are more likely to acquire symbolic capital as well. Possessing lesser volumes of cultural capital, the young people leaving school had less legitimacy in this field and, therefore, little or no symbolic capital. Perceiving close associations with education and educational research, these young people not only had less cultural capital to convert into narrative capital when invited into the sub-field of research into higher education, but also less symbolic capital.

Symbolic value can also attach itself more directly to narrative capital. This is not just the believability of the well told tale, the authority of the carefully crafted phrase (so beloved of academic writers) when set against the stammerings of someone with little to say or fewer means of saying it (nor is this an idle point: in a research environment where time is increasingly money and therefore in short supply, those who may need more support in telling their stories are likely to have less opportunity to do so and to do so well). So the better the story and the better the storytelling – or the more effective the strategic deployment of the narrative capital – the greater the likelihood that this additional symbolic capital will be attached to it.

This is where the life historian, seeking to transform the life story into the life history, must play her part because, as suggested here, the life story may be fragmentary and inarticulate; and if it is not much of a story, then it cannot tell much of a life. Here, the life historian constructs the narrative that makes sense of the data in whatever form (Polkinghorne, 1995) so that 'the narrative is the product of the analysis and not the starting point' (Griffiths and Macleod, forthcoming). Whilst this is not a chapter on how to do narrative research, it should, perhaps, be added that we perceived the symbolic capital of our participants in terms of their legitimate participation in the research and that the research was geared towards getting them to tell their stories. With the young people who had left school, for example, their stories went on to address other manifestations of capital and as they moved away from talking about events and institutions that had not valued them – that is, as they talked towards other social fields in which they perceived themselves to have greater legitimacy and where they therefore acquired more symbolic capital – they began to deploy greater narrative capital. The symbolic capital they acquired from the legitimate telling of their tales gave them the 'access ... to humanity' (Bourdieu, 2000: 241) that leads towards the concept of narrative capability.

Narrative Capability

The capability approach developed by Amartya Sen (1992, 1999) and Martha Nussbaum (2000, 2006) can appear deceptively simple with its concern to address the substantive freedoms individuals have to choose and lead lives they value and have reason to value. Narrative capability – the real opportunities individuals have to tell their stories – is of fundamental importance to the capability approach because it enables the articulation of what is valued and the recognition of the truly human life (see also Bonvin and Farvaque, 2005; Phelps, 2006). Yet if the foundations of narrative research indicate the importance of narrative capability, the unequal distribution of narrative capital can significantly inhibit it. These difficulties, as well as the complexities of the capability approach, can be gauged by briefly contextualising its origins as a response to the shortcomings of commodities-based and utilitarian assessments of human well-being.

From a capability perspective, commodities (which include goods in the Rawlsian sense and capital in the Bourdieusian sense described above) only have value inasmuch as they enable individuals to make use of them in the pursuit and achievement of a valued life. Thus, turning to an example that frequently appears in the capability literature, a bicycle has no value to someone who cannot ride it because she is disabled, because there are no suitable cycle routes or because there may be laws or mores prohibiting women from cycling. Moreover, human diversity means that we may require different volumes of any given commodity to achieve the same level of well-being. Another well rehearsed example that illustrates this problem of conversion factors is the breastfeeding mother who requires a significantly greater calorific intake to nourish herself and her child than, say, a pensioner leading a very sedentary life. None of this is to suggest that commodities and capital have no value; and both Sen and Nussbaum clearly indicate that being well off can make a significant contribution to well-being. However, commodities cannot be the sole measure of that well-being and so, from a capability perspective, the focus has to be on 'the freedoms generated by commodities, rather than on the commodities seen on their own' (Sen, 1999: 74).

Individuals may, therefore, have reserves of narrative capital but be unable to make use of them – particularly if a necessary condition of this narrative capability is the freedom to be listened to. The plight of graduate refugees seeking to validate their higher level qualifications illustrates these difficulties. They have stories to tell but if their English language skills are poor then they are unlikely to be heard (Watts and Bridges, 2005; Watts, 2007a) and the anti-immigration sentiments of some national newspapers means they may not want to speak up. Continuing Bourdieu's economic metaphor, their capital is invested in a foreign currency that they cannot spend in the UK. Similarly, the young people we worked with who had chosen not to progress to higher education did not necessarily have enough narrative capital to make themselves heard above the clamour of greater volumes generated by governmental admonishments to do so. Thus, although both groups have narrative capital, neither has sufficient capital to have their narratives recognised or respected and so, from a capability perspective, their capital alone cannot be a measure of their well-being.

A further problem with commodity- and capital-based approaches to well-being is that the lack of capital can lead to the adaptation of preferences. The capability critique of utilitarianism centres upon the insidious nature of adaptive preferences and concerns the failure of preference-satisfaction based assessments of well-being to acknowledge the human tendency to adapt preferences under unfavourable circumstances (Zimmerman, 2003; Bridges, 2006). Such self-assessments of well-being are therefore likely to be distorted by deprivation and blur the distinction between 'what people really prefer and what they are made to prefer' (Teschl and Comin, 2005: 236). Sen, for example, notes that the constraints which adaptive preferences place upon individuals lead to the misrepresentation of the true circumstances of those such as the 'thoroughly deprived person, leading a very reduced life' who accepts hardship with 'non-grumbling resignation' and makes 'great efforts to take pleasure in small mercies and to cut down personal desires to modest – 'realistic' – proportions' (1992: 55) and Nussbaum (2000) extensively cites Rabindranath Tagore's 'Letter from a wife' to illustrate the 'non-grumbling resignation' of the eponymous wife to her extreme deprivation.

Under such circumstances of chronic subjugation, the individual does not necessarily want or see the need to give voice to her narrative. Nor does she necessarily perceive any value in her story and, because she has not known or cannot see any alternative, she expresses a preference for the reduced and silenced life that does not require narrative capital. This is not a matter of having nothing to say but of narrative capital not being valued because she has no desire to seek her own advantage over others. This adaptation to resignation (Teschl and Comin, 2005) has, for example, been a significant feature of our work with refugees: ground down by the refusal of others to hear them, many of them had simply accepted their lot and had then subsequently expressed their preference for the easier life it allowed them. However, adaptive preferences can be challenged through the investment of appropriate support and capital (Watts, 2007b) and we found that some of the refugees who had slumped into their adaptive preferences were prepared to raise their aspirations because of something as simple as having someone listen to their stories.

Such investments notwithstanding, within the capability approach mere preference is an insufficient basis for evaluating individual well-being. Not only must the individual value whatever aspect of her life is under evaluative scrutiny, she must have reason to value it. This has two implications. The first is that there should be individual justification for whatever is held to be of value (that is, there is an informed valuation). The second is that there is a good reason to value it because it is constitutive of the truly human life (Nussbaum, 2000, 2006). Sen and Nussbaum offer different understandings of what, for the purpose of capability assessments, constitutes this truly human life. For Sen, what comprises it should be identified through a democratic process of open and informed debate (Sen, 1999; Alkire, 2002; Deneulin, 2006) whilst Nussbaum turns to a list of central human functionings generated by a meta-debate that takes place beyond the immediate evaluation (2000). Although they may have a significant influence upon the conduct of capability assessments, these differences do not matter here because they share the same pertinent point: narrative capability – that is, the substantive freedom to deploy one's narrative capital in order to be heard and acknowledged – is vital. If the individual's voice is not heard, she cannot contribute to the debate and, moreover, she may find herself acquiescing in the unchallenged value attributed to unjust hierarchies (Bonvin and Farvaque, 2005; Phelps, 2006; Watts, 2007b).

To address the concern that self-assessments of well-being may be subject to adaptive preferences, the capability approach requires well-being assessments to take into account what an individual would do under different circumstances – or, in Sen's words, what she would do if she controlled the levers of power (1992: 64-69). This premise of counterfactuality, though, is 'philosophically puzzling' and if, in general, 'we are trying to elucidate a concept ... it is not a good idea to invoke counterfactual assumptions. This would be seeking to elucidate the less obscure by the more obscure' (Everitt and Fisher, 1995: 35). However, capability analyses sidestep this epistemological puzzle by making interpersonal comparisons. Would the 'thoroughly deprived person, leading a very reduced life' choose to accept her hardship with non-grumbling resignation if she were higher up the stratified society? Would she speak up if she had greater narrative capital? What would she say if she had a voice? How much clearer would her voice be if it were amplified by the symbolic capital generated by legitimation of her presence in the relevant field? How would this influence our understanding of what she valued and had reason to value? And how would this then influence our understanding of her well-being?

Enhancing Narrative Capability

At least some answers can be gleaned from the three studies above. The Oxbridge students, telling tales about the deployment of their cultural capital in the field of higher education, clearly had sufficient narrative capital to give them the narrative capability to tell those stories and to tell them well. They therefore are the point of reference for the interpersonal comparisons that enable the counterfactual well-being assessments of the other participants.

What would have enabled the refugees to tell their tales as well? Unlike the students, they typically lacked the resources (here the cultural and linguistic capitals) that would have given them the substantive freedoms to choose and lead the lives they valued and had reason to value, that is, within the parameters of the research, the opportunities to engage with higher education. Capability assessments of well-being enable the identification of the resources individuals need to provide them with those freedoms; and here, in terms of the freedom to engage with higher education, it is clear that they required the investment of these cultural and linguistic capitals. Moreover, at least some of these refugees lacked the narrative capital they needed to participate fully in the research that otherwise would have given them the opportunity to articulate these valued ways of living.

Here, it would seem, there is a responsibility upon the researcher to provide them with the necessary resources that make up for that deficit of narrative capital (and, apart from this ethical obligation, under such circumstances, and without such additional capital investment, the narrative research is likely to be very thin). In this research, the investment took various forms from carefully rephrasing questions to providing translators but it was all geared towards providing them with the real opportunities they needed to deploy whatever narrative capital they had in order to express themselves.

The young people leaving school provide a different and more conceptual problem to resolve. What would enable them to tell their tales as well as the Oxbridge students? As with the refugees, we provided greater supportive and encouraging interventions. The real problem for them, though, was that the narrative field of research overlapped with the educational field of schooling and they had neither valued nor had reason to value that schooling (Watts and Bridges, 2006). That is, what disadvantaged them when talking about their formal education was the very focus of the research. When they were given the opportunity to talk about those things they valued and had reason to value – rather than those things they had been told they should value and have reason to value – the narrative field shifted and over-lapped with other fields in which they were able to recognise their legitimacy; and the forms of capital in those fields transmuted into the narrative capital they needed to tell their stories.

Conclusion

The young people leaving school were given the opportunity to tell their stories and this enhanced narrative capital allowed them to challenge the hierarchically determined presumption that they had low aspirations because they were not progressing to higher education. They had been given the narrative capability they had required to deploy the narrative capital they possessed in order to narrate the stories of their lives. Capability is concerned with the substantive freedoms the individual has to choose and lead a life she values and has reason to value. It is necessary to question the extent to which the freedom to articulate those choices may be restricted by hierarchical power structures that presume socially constructed values and that, moreover, limit opportunity to talk even when invited to do so. Life histories have the potential to resolve this by providing research participants with the freedom to tell their stories and by contextualising those stories to identify and confront the socially constructed hierarchies of power that may otherwise inhibit the telling of tales.

The enhancement of narrative capability requires us to pay attention to the bigger story of which education may be only a small part. But we must also pay attention to the participant's ability to tell a story. It may not be enough to let them struggle through the story unaided. We may be able to develop an understanding of their lives from stumbling speech and from silences but this is not necessarily enough. Giving voice to our research participants, particularly those with low volumes of narrative capital, must therefore mean more than simply letting them speak (although this legitimation may be all they require). It must be about understanding; and they may need support to articulate and understand their own lives. Moreover, this support must acknowledge their own values if we are to avoid the hegemonic imposition of other lives, other stories and other values upon them. We come back to life histories as a means of talking truth and confronting power because they enable us to contextualise the stories we are told and to understand them from the perspective of the storyteller.

References

Alkire, S (2002) *Valuing Freedoms: Sen's capability approach and poverty.* Oxford: Oxford University Press

Bonvin, J-M and Farvaque, N (2005) What informational basis for assessing job-seekers?: capabilities vs. preferences. *Review of Social Economy* 63(2) p269-289.

Bourdieu, P (1988) *Homo Academicus.* Cambridge: Polity Press

Bourdieu, P (1991) *Language and Symbolic Power.* Cambridge: Polity Press

Bourdieu, P (1993) *Sociology in Question.* London: Sage

Bourdieu, P (1996) *The State Nobility.* Cambridge: Polity Press

Bourdieu, P (1998) *Practical Reason.* Cambridge: Polity Press

Bourdieu, P (2000) *Pascalian Meditations.* Cambridge: Polity Press

Bourdieu, P and Passeron, J-C (1977) *Reproduction in Education, Society and Culture.* London: Sage

Bourdieu, P and Wacquant, L (1992) *An Invitation to Reflexive Sociology.* Cambridge: Polity Press

Bridges, D (2006) Adaptive preference, justice and identity in the context of widening participation in higher education. *Ethics and Education* 1(1) p15-28

Bruner, J (1986) *Actual Minds, Possible Worlds.* Cambridge, Ma: Harvard University Press

Deneulin, S (2006) *The Capability Approach and the Praxis of Development.* Basingstoke: Palgrave Macmillan

Everitt, N and Fisher, A (1995) *Modern Epistemology: a new introduction.* New York: McGraw-Hill

Gillies, V (2006) Working class mothers and school life: exploring the role of emotional capital. *Gender and Education* 18(3) p281-293

Goodson, I and Sikes, P (2001) *Life History Research in Educational Settings: learning from lives.* Buckingham: Open University Press

Goodson, I. and Walker, R (1991) *Biography, Identity and Schooling: episodes in educational research.* London: Falmer Press

Griffiths, M and Macleod, G (forthcoming) Personal narratives and policy: never the twain? *Journal of Philosophy of Education* forthcoming

Lieblich, A, Tuval-Mashiach, R and Zilber, T (1998) *Narrative Research: reading, analysis, and interpretation.* Thousand Oaks, Ca: Sage

Miller, R (2000) *Researching Life Stories and Family Histories.* London: Sage

Moore, R (2004) Cultural capital: objective probability and the cultural arbitrary. *British Journal of Sociology of Education* 25(4) p445-56

Nussbaum, N (2000) *Women and Human Development: the capabilities approach.* Cambridge University Press: Cambridge

Nussbaum, N (2006) *Frontiers of Justice: disability, nationality, species membership.* Cambridge, MA: the Belknap Press

Phelps, T (2006) Narrative capability. In S Deneulin, M Nebel and N Sagovsky (eds) *Transforming Unjust Structures.* Dordrecht: Springer

Polkinghorne, D (1995) Narrative configuration in qualitative analysis. In J Hatch and R Wisniewski (eds) *Life History and Narrative.* London: Falmer Press

Reay, D (2000) A useful extension of Bourdieu's conceptual framework? Emotional capital as a way of understanding mother' involvement in their children's education? *Sociological Review* 48(4) p568-585

Roberts, B (2002) *Biographical Research.* Buckingham: Open University Press

Sen, A (1992) *Inequality Reexamined.* Oxford University Press: Oxford

Sen, A (1999) *Development as Freedom.* Oxford University Press: Oxford

Shilling, C (2004) Physical capital and situated action: a new direction for corporeal socio-logy. *British Journal of Sociology of Education* 25(4) p473-88

Teschl, M and Comin, F (2005) Adaptive preferences and capabilities: some preliminary conceptual explorations. *Review of Social Economy,* 63(2) p229-247

Watts, M (2002) *Everything that I am, Oxbridge is the Opposite.* London: the Sutton Trust

Watts, M (2007a) Capability, identity and access to elite universities. *Prospero* 13(3) p22-33

Watts, M (2007b) Widening participation in higher education for refugees and asylum seekers. *Race Equality Teaching* 25(3) p44-48

Watts, M and Bridges, D (2004) *Whose Aspirations? What Achievement? An investigation of the life and lifestyle aspirations of 16-19 year olds outside the formal educational system.* Cambridge: Association of Universities in the East of England

Watts, M and Bridges, D (2005) *Higher education opportunities for refugees, asylum seekers and migrant workers in the East of England.* Cambridge: Association of Universities in the East of England

Watts, M and Bridges, D (2006) The value of non-participation in higher education. *Journal of Education Policy* 21(3) p267-290

Zimmerman, D (2003) Sour grapes, self-abnegation and character building: non-respon-sibility and responsibility for self-induced preferences. *The Monist* 86(2) p220-241

8

Speaking Truth to Power: Edward Said and the work of the intellectual

FAZAL RIZVI

Throughout his distinguished career the question of what it means to be an intellectual was something of a preoccupation with Edward Said. Each of his essays, interviews and books returned in one way or another to this key question, as he struggled to examine the ways in which it might be possible for intellectuals to promote the causes of democracy and social justice, without getting co-opted within the structures of power and identity politics on the one hand and disciplinary rigidities and organisational systems on the other. In his analysis, Said was as fearless as he was profound. His writings exemplified that rare synthesis of clarity and political commitment, a combination that did not always guarantee conceptual consistency but always exemplified civic courage. He insisted on the need to think honestly and clearly, as well as creatively and critically, about issues of knowledge and power, of theory and practice and of culture and imperialism. He stressed the importance of thinking historically in ways that were at once local and global. He worked with a range of theoretical traditions, thus avoiding intellectual fads and fashions. He insisted that the role of the intellectual was to 'speak truth to power'.

In this chapter, I want to examine some aspects of this much quoted, though inherently complex, idiom. Who can speak, how, under what conditions, and with what consequences – and with what purpose? What might truth consist in, especially within normative realms where there are competing senses of justice and where universality is always elusive? When is it appropriate to confront power, and when is it strategic to occupy what Gramsci (1973) called 'a war of position'? These questions were never too far away from Said's intellectual gaze, but they produced answers that remain highly contested, not least because the humanism upon which they are based invokes a universalism that conflicts with his insistence on the particular and on 'worldliness'. The capacity for intellectuals to say anything relevant about their society cannot, he maintains, dispense with the concept of worldliness, for without worldliness they have no world from which, and to which, to speak. Said is thus highly critical of academic specialisations, which often speak to themselves, becoming removed from the political realities of contemporary society.

Sceptical of fixed positions from which to speak, no matter how seemingly progressive, Said underlines the importance of contingency in both theoretical and political deliberations. Even his humanism is provisional. Responding to his critics (eg Clifford, 1980), Said maintains that: 'it should be possible to be critical of humanism in the name of humanism' (Said, 2004: 10). Said refuses to view social theory in its narrow sense, but insists that it needs to be grounded within a political struggle that is spatially and historically specific. For him, intellectual work must always be viewed as tentative and strategic, working against the illusions of dualities and certainties. Indeed, as Said (1994a: xii) insists, in his Reith lectures, intellectuals are 'those figures whose public performances can neither be predicted nor compelled into some slogan, orthodox party line, or fixed dogma'. In distinguishing themselves from 'the insiders, experts, coteries and professionals', intellectuals, he argues, need to question 'patriotic nationalism, corporate thinking, and a sense of class, racial or gender privilege' (p.xiii). Without such critical reflexivity, they lose their capacity to 'speak truth to power'.

In a post-September 11 world, this is a risk that has become especially evident, as political caution replaces criticality, and as political orthodoxy silences alternative voices. Let me illustrate this point with a story. In September 2004, I attended a meeting at a mosque in the small university town in the United States in which I live and work. The mosque has a reputation of being an inclusive place, which sponsors many events designed to promote, through inter-faith dialogue, a better understanding of Islam and its diverse cultural traditions. In recent years, these meetings have become more frequent, as Muslim communities throughout the United States and elsewhere have become increasingly drawn into thinking about the ways in which Islam configures within the contemporary geo-politics so dramatically reshaped by the horrific events of September 11 and its aftermath. I went to the meeting in order to find out how American Muslims and others viewed the popular representations of Islam and what potential they saw in inter-faith dialogue. Given the line-up of speakers, I expected a vigorous discussion about the ways in which Islam was being demonised for the actions of a small minority of deranged Muslims, and what was needed to promote greater inter-cultural understanding.

Disappointingly, however, the meeting turned out to be a tame affair, with none of the four speakers representing different religious traditions saying anything critically new. They mostly reiterated the familiar sentiments about the need to respect religious diversity, to live in harmony, and other such slogans of liberal multiculturalism. It was evident that some of the speakers at least, held back their sentiments. This much was clearly revealed to me at the reception after the meeting, when, in a private conversation, one of the speakers, an elderly retired professor who was born in Pakistan but had lived in the United States for more than thirty years, became much more animated and forthright in his comments. In Urdu, he confided that: '*Ab hum bol nahin sakte*', translated literally, 'now we are unable to speak'. I found this sentiment intriguing, not least because of the stark disjuncture between his public speaking and his private views, which were full not only of resignation and melancholy but also of considerable fear. He was deeply pessimistic about the future. He spoke of his despair at what Tariq Ali (2003) has referred to as the 'clash of fundamentalisms'. He predicted that relations between Islamic communities and others around the world are going to get much worse. The contrast between his private and public utterances indicated also that he had lost confidence in the public spaces that might have once enabled him to speak more openly and freely.

Since that meeting, I have often thought about the professor's contention: '*Ab hum bol nahin sakte*'. I have wondered about his use of the term '*Ab*', meaning 'now', which suggested that he believed that sometime in the past relations between Islam and others were somehow better, clearly raising the issue of the politics relating to their deterioration, and also to the question of how this deterioration could be arrested and overcome. I have tried to understand why the professor was so timid in his public enunciations yet so bold in private. He clearly regarded himself, and was regarded by others, as an intellectual, but was reluctant to engage in the kind of critical practice Said would have considered necessary for imagining and enacting the possibilities of inter-faith dialogue. And finally, his use of the term '*hum*' suggested that he regarded me as a part of his community — the 'we' to which '*hum*' referred. Such a binary was clearly based on an identity politics, which could not envisage a 'third space' (Bhabha, 1994) for me — beyond or between Islam and non-Islam. It implied a distinction between a private discourse for those considered the insiders and a public discourse for the rest. In short, it was this identity politics that defined what he was able to say, to whom and how.

The view that Muslims in the United States and elsewhere can no longer speak – not literally of course but politically — without risks is of course widely held. The Council for American-Islamic relations has repeatedly asserted that the popular discourses of the so-called 'Islamic threat' have forced many Muslims into political silence, while, in the United Kingdom, the Islamic Human Rights Commission has reported a climate of fear that exists in many Muslim communities. Regardless of whether this fear is justified or not, such claims have clearly given rise to a new cultural politics of speaking.

In her much-cited essay, 'Can the Subaltern Speak?', Gayatri Spivak (1987) discusses some of the issues associated with the old colonial politics of speaking. She argues that in the colonial contexts, political silence did not always mean the subalterns' compliance; and also that their ability to speak was always contingent upon their preparedness to operate within the hegemonic norms of a society. In this way, colonialism constructed political subjects who spoke only in the permitted and prescribed forms. The new politics of speaking appears much more complex, based on strategic decisions people make before saying things that might otherwise be construed as unsympathetic to the nation and contrary to its security interests. A new language of security thus now defines the parameters of political conversation, and even intellectual work.

Said recognises such constraints on our speaking but nonetheless insists that an intellectual is 'set apart, someone able to speak the truth to power, a crusty, eloquent, fantastically courageous and angry individual for whom no worldly power is too big and imposing to be criticised and pointedly taken to task' (1994a: 8). The determination to speak openly and with courage, argues Said, is a most basic pre-condition of a free, democratic and socially just society. But does this mean that those who do not speak truth to power are timid, or some-how anti-intellectual? In my view, this would be a harsh assessment indeed, for people are only able to speak in political conditions in which they are convinced that the public airing of their grievances will not prove counter-productive and that their interests will not be harmed by their willingness to speak openly and honestly.

The professor at the inter-faith meeting had clearly decided to remain publicly silent, for the fear of becoming politically marked. His was a dilemma confronted by many Muslims living in communities where they are in a minority. They are repeatedly asked to condemn terror-ism but when they do their voices are not always heard, as the popu-lar media continues to utter repeatedly the same stereotypes, and many law-makers find it politically useful to perpetuate nationalist sentiments couched in a new language of war against terror. In such a context, many Muslims, even intellectuals, feel it best to become in-visible, in the hope that things will get better soon. Yet they realise that this invisibility has its costs, for it makes them feel further alienated and marginalised.

It is not hard therefore to understand their reasons for despair and silence. We live in a world that demands simple solutions to complex problems, clear and unambiguous responses to the new social and cul-tural challenges. Since September 11, people want their governments to make them feel secure, and punish severely those who are identified as their enemies. They are even prepared to concede many of their democratic rights, with the expectation that the government will look after their security. With this new political settlement between people and governments, a great deal is left unsaid, as the definitions of we and our enemies are seldom subjected to critical scrutiny. Implicitly discouraged in this new climate is any analysis of the most fundamental normativity upon which the nation is imagined (Anderson, 1983). Assumptions thus made have the consequence of de-politicising political debates about identity and difference, as well as about policy measures needed to counter the threats of terrorism. As Jayasuriya (2002: 131) argues, under the cloak of security, governments around the world are able to usher in a debilitating form of 'anti-politics' that sidelines contentious matters.

People fear being labelled unpatriotic or being against the presumed national interest. This produces effects already apparent in a number of countries that otherwise view themselves as democratic, where self-censorship in the media has made honest discussions of the political sources of terrorism extremely difficult, if not impossible. This self-censorship has begun to define the boundaries of popular discourses about identity, difference and the nation. Moreover, and perhaps more invidiously, the technical language of security, couched in terms of 'risk', has occluded important issues of conflict and power. Power itself has assumed a new character that is beyond reproach. Spurred on by a new climate of fear, an almost exclusive conception of security has emerged, which places less emphasis on social and historical causes of insecurity and more on policing its citizens, especially those who were already marginalised. As Jayasuriya (2002: 140) observes, 'new forms of risk management involve applying risk profiles to a set of relationships, institutions, and even geographic sites, rather than endeavouring to manage or transform the behaviour of people'.

Perhaps the main problem with this new language of security is that it encourages and legitimises absolutist definitions. Far too often, words like 'war', 'justice', 'victory' and indeed 'security' are used by politicians and the popular media as if they have single, uniform and incontestable meanings. Popular slogans such as 'crusade against the enemies of democracy' and 'eliminating evil from the world' serve only to hinder democratic debate about the causes, expressions and outcomes of terrorism and a whole variety of possible remedies that could address the new challenges. Paradoxically, in its broad linguistic structure, this absolutism is broadly similar to that used by militant Islam. It consists in a language of moral certainty and political absolutes. Steven Lukes and Nadia Urbinati (2001) have called it a 'war between absolutes'. It assumes that Islam speaks with a singular voice. But in so doing, it not only overlooks the facts of the cultural and political construction of Islam but also of the perspective from which this construction is articulated. But as Said has noted, 'cultures are too intermingled, their contents and histories too interdependent and hybrid, for surgical separation into large and mostly ideological oppositions like Orient and Occident' (1994b: xii).

As Lukes and Urbinati note, 'the new terrorism therefore has an insidious power, one which derives from the non-political character of its language and objectives and which encourages its victims to use the same language. And in the victims' traditions there are, of course, ample resources of religious dogmatism from which to draw'. This dogmatism invites the translation of all human and social phenomena into a religious language: 'just' becomes 'good', 'wrong' becomes 'evil', 'the political adversary' becomes 'the Infidel'. From a democratic point of view, this makes dialogue across religious traditions extremely difficult. This is so because such binaries increase the polarisation and conflict across communities. As Nira Yuval-Davis (2001) points out, in times of war, the pressure to conform to binary oppositions – to absorb them not only into our language but also our very thought processes is especially great. Furthermore, the attempts to divide the world into civilisations become highly plausible: 'us' and 'them'. Indeed, the clash of civilisations thesis, put forward by Samuel Huntington (1996), trades on this plausibility, by positing two unbridgeable civilisational blocs, religiously and culturally apart. This makes hybrid positions, and those that seek to transcend the binary, difficult to imagine, let alone realise.

In contrast, for Said, a cultural tradition cannot be understood except as a complex and diverse religious system, shaped not only by its own metaphysical postulates and ethical demands but perhaps even more so by the circumstances of its colonial past and its politics in the modern world. Over the past century alone, Islam, for example, like most other communities, has had to address internal tensions as well as external pressures. In the era of globalisation, it has had to come to terms with new economic, social and cultural formations. Both within and beyond Islam, conflict therefore has unmistakable political dimension, and cannot be explained in cultural terms alone. Yet the 'culturalisation' of conflict, as suggested by Huntington, is as wrong as it is dangerous. It is wrong because while the origins of some disputes are certainly cultural, prolonged conflict is always much more complex, involving factors that are not only cultural but also economic, political and ideological. Nor is it possible to differentiate one civilisation from another in such an holistic and abstract manner. As Said (2001) has pointed out, Huntington, has made civilisations into 'shut down and sealed off' entities, overlooking the exchange, cross-fertilisation and sharing that has always been responsible for cultural change within all communities, not only as a result of currents and counter currents of trade but also colonialism.

Perhaps a more serious problem with Huntington's thesis is its lack of theoretical reflexivity. It does not examine the perspective from which it is itself articulated. Nor does it explore its political consequences in a world in which cultural representations are highly contested, and in which globalisation is increasingly propelling cultures towards mutual interaction, hybridising cultural experiences, and creating multiple positions from which people are now able to speak. Huntington's analysis risks the danger of both absolutism and specialisation. As a specialised discourse, it is unable to take into account the profound cultural transformations that are currently taking place, and cannot therefore speak to the pressing political concerns of contemporary societies. And, paradoxically, as an absolutist discourse, it is easily utilised by groups committed to an inflexible and un-accommodating identity politics. In both terms, it runs counter to the role Said envisages for intellectuals.

According to Said (1994a: 11), an intellectual has 'a specific public role that cannot be reduced simply to being a faceless professional', articulating abstract theses. Things intellectuals say should matter, because they have a faculty for representing, embodying, articulating a message, a view, an attitude, philosophy or opinion to, as well as for, a 'public'[1]. This role of the intellectual implies raising embarrassing questions publicly, confronting orthodoxy and dogma, avoiding co-option by government or corporations, and most importantly, representing the people and issues usually forgotten or hidden. In this sense, intellectual spirit is in opposition rather than in accommodation. But since intellectual work can always be misused, reflexivity is an essential feature of the worldliness of the texts that intellectuals interpret and produce. The world and its links to the text and the critic is thus crucial to Said's perception of the value of intellectual work. He argues that intellectuals face a set of concrete choices and while they represent something to their audiences, they represent themselves to themselves as well. This means that they act according to an idea or representation informed not only by their disciplinary traditions but also by their values and commitment.

To develop his notion of an intellectual, Said draws both from Gramsci's (1973) idea of an 'organic intellectual' and Julien Benda's (1980) definition of intellectuals as that small group of academic elites who constitute the conscience of human kind. For Benda, the aim of intellectual work is essentially not the pursuit of practical ends but the practice of an art or a science or metaphysical speculation. In this sense, Benda's conception is as exclusive as Gramsci's is inclusive. The aim of intellectual work, for Gramsci, is not the development of abstractions but an entire social movement through which to organise interests and gain political power and control in order to challenge capitalism in its various hegemonic forms. Gramsci believes that organic intellectuals should be actively involved in society, engaged in constant struggle to change minds and expand influence. So while Benda's notion of intellectuals is elitist, Gramsci is democratic. Said (1993: 15) argues however that this contrast need not be viewed as contradictory, but that intellectual work can serve multiple functions, of both interpreting the world and engaging with it. He says that being an intellectual 'involves what Foucault once called 'a relentless erudition", but that it also demands 'a sense of the dramatic and the insurgent, making a great deal of one's rare opportunities to speak'.

In this way, Said is not opposed to erudition and disciplinary rigour, but he is clear in his warning about the trap of those practices of specialisation, a cult of professional expertise, that makes intellectual work marginal to the urgent political concerns. He is highly critical of those academic practices that have isolated 'textuality from the circumstances, the events, the physical senses that made it possible and render it intelligible as the result of human work' (Said 1983: 4). In so doing, Said says:

> Contemporary criticism has retreated from its constituency, the citizens of modern society, who have been left to the hands of 'free' market forces, multinational corporations, the manipulations of consumer appetites. A precious jargon has grown up, and its

formidable complexities obscure the social realities that, strange though it may seem, encourage a scholarship of 'modes of excellence' very far from daily life. (Said, 1983: 4)

Said contends that criticism should not be used to validate the *status quo*, but rather, to underscore how texts are connected with 'the existential actualities of human life' (p.5). What makes texts possible are 'the realities of power and authority, as well as the resistances offered by men, women, and social movements to institutions, authorities and orthodoxies' (p.5). Therefore, criticism should be focused on those realities and practices that are outside and beyond the *status quo*.

He calls this 'secular criticism', which as Ashcroft and Ahluwalia (1999: 30) characterise it, 'dispenses with priestly and abstruse specialisation in favour of a breadth of interest and what he (Said) calls amateurism of approach, avoiding the retreat of intellectual work from the actual society in which it occurs'. In this way, secular criticism implies an awareness of its context, a sensitive and strategic response to the dominant cultural formations. According to Said (1983: 15), the individual consciousness is not only a cultural product, but is also 'a historical and social actor in it'. So, the key question for Said (1983: 24) is:

What does it mean to have a critical consciousness if ... the intellectual's situation is a worldly one and yet, by virtue of that worldliness itself, the intellectual's social identity should involve something more than strengthening those aspects of the culture that require mere affirmation and orthodox compliancy from its members?

A critical consciousness needs to be aware of the pressures exerted upon the intellectuals' work by their culture, to which they are bound filiatively (by birth, or nationality), as well as by the method or system they have acquired affiliatively (by social and political beliefs, economic and political circumstances, deliberate effort and willed consideration) (Said, 1983: 25). It needs to stand between culture and system, which implies 'to stand close to ... a concrete reality about which political, moral and social judgments have to be made and, if not only made, then exposed and demystified'. In short, the critic needs to make sense of the political, social and human values implied in the reading, production, and transmission of every text without reducing it to a doctrine or political position. The critic should disbelieve totalising concepts, reject orthodox habits of mind and express discontent with reified objects (Said, 1983: 29). More importantly, 'criticism must think of itself as life-enhancing and constitutively opposed to every form of tyranny, domination and abuse; its social goals are non-coercive knowledge produced in the interest of human freedom' (Said, 1983: 26).

In this way, Said's notion of intellectual work is fundamentally grounded within a normative framework. In his Reith lectures, he characterises this as being based on a set of 'universal principles: that all human beings are entitled to expect decent standards of behaviour concerning freedom and justice from worldly power or nations, and that deliberate or inadvertent violations of these standards need to be testified and fought against courageously' (Said, 1994a: 12). Speaking truth to power is not an end in itself but rather 'the goal of speaking the truth is ... mainly to project a better state of affairs, one that corresponds more closely to a set of moral principles – peace, reconciliation, abatement of suffering – applied to the known facts' (Said, 1994a: 99-100). Further, the intellectual's goal consists in inducing 'a change in the moral climate whereby aggression is seen as such, the unjust punishment of peoples or individuals is either prevented or given up, the recognition of rights and democratic freedoms is established as a norm for everyone, not invidiously for a selected few' (Said, 1994a: 100). In order to be able to 'speak the truth to power', intellectuals need to avoid those habits of mind that seek to avoid difficult or controversial ideas or positions and that destroy a passionate intellectual life. Speaking the truth to power implies 'weighing the alternatives, picking the right one, and then intelligently representing it where it can do the most good and cause the right change' (Said, 1994a: 102).

For Said, the moral good is derived from his distinctive understanding of humanist principles. Said recognises that moral rationalities are differently interpreted and articulated, but insists that intercultural articulation, even debate, requires a collective search for a range of moral principles that are born of humanity itself. In a book published after his death, *Humanism and Democratic Criticism* (2004), Said focuses on 'the relevance and future of humanism in contemporary life', and views it 'as a usable praxis for intellectuals and academics who want to know what they are doing, what they are committed to as scholars, and who want also to connect these principles to the world in which they live as citizens' (Said, 2004: 6). He argues that it is necessary to highlight the importance of humanism at a time when the global economy and the cultural landscape are undergoing drastic trans-formations. Even when he may be hesitant about the contemporary usefulness of terms such as 'humanistic' or 'the humanities', Said thus undertakes the task of understanding humanism 'in light of its past and of its probable future' (p.7). This is because for Said humanism is linked to ideals of justice and equality. For him, 'humanistic ideals of liberty and learning still supply most disadvantaged people with the energy to resist [injustice] and to try to overturn despotism and tyranny' (Said, 2004: 10). It is moreover possible to be critical, he argues, of humanism in the name of humanism, and that, schooled in its abuses by the experience of Eurocentrism and empire, one could still fashion a different kind of humanism that was cosmopolitan.

At the centre of this kind of humanism is the secular notion that the historical world is made by men and women, and that it is possible to understand this world rationally, as well as historically and relationally. Historical knowledge, he argues, is based in the human being's capacity to make knowledge, even as we recognise that the human mind is fallible, and thus, 'there is always something radically incomplete, insufficient, provisional, disputable, and arguable about humanistic knowledge' (Said, 2004: 12). In other words, Said denies the existence of neutral, objective and non-historical knowledge, and insists that 'the subjective element in humanistic knowledge and prac-tice has to be recognised and in some way reckoned with' (*ibid*: 12).

He (2004: 21-22) claims therefore that 'to understand humanism at all is to understand it as democratic, open to all classes and back-grounds, and as a process of unending disclosure, discovery, self-criti-cism, and liberation'. Never before, he insists, has there been a greater need for intercultural dialogue that is based on a view that the useful-ness of the humanities lies in their ability 'to show us history as an agonistic process still being made, rather than finished and settled once and for all'. This open-ended view of humanism implies that the continuous process of self-understanding and self-realisation is not only important for white, male, American and European, but for everyone.

In this way, Said links humanism to criticism as, for him, humanism is critique, which is directed at the state of affairs that is historically grounded, relationally defined, reflexively nuanced and imaginatively projected; and that gathers its force and relevance by its democratic, secular, and open character. For Said, an emphasis on such epistemic virtues should lie at the heart of all education designed 'to make more things available to critical scrutiny as the product of human labour, human energies for emancipation and enlightenment, and, just as importantly, human misreadings and misinterpretations of the collective past and present' (Said, 2004: 22). If this is so, then education is now constitutively in need of revision, rethinking and revitalisation. This is because the:

> mental and aesthetic universe that was linguistically, formally, and epistemologically grounded in the European and North Atlantic world of the classics, the church, and empire, in their traditions, languages and masterworks ... has been replaced by a much more varied and complex world with many contradictory, even antinomian and antithetical currents running within it (Said, 2004: 44-45).

As a significant number of dissenting voices in marginalised and oppositional sectors (ie feminist, ethnic, postcolonial studies) emerge, the need of rethinking and revitalising the humanities in particular but education more generally becomes evident.

But such re-thinking and revitalisation is impossible unless we learn to speak truth to power. Education has always served multiple purposes, some designed to reproduce existing patterns of power, while others are intended to question them. Education can serve the markets and self-interests of people, as it has increasingly been re-designed to do. But it can equally produce intellectuals who see critique as a form of democratic freedom and who learn the continuous practice of questioning and of accumulating knowledge that is open to, rather than in denial of, the 'historical realities of the post-Cold War world, its early colonial formation, and the frighteningly global reach of the last remaining superpower of today' (Said, 2004: 45). It should indeed be possible for a new humanist education to show how, in the past, cultural traditions have interacted with each other and can, more importantly, continue to interact in peaceful ways' (p.49).

In other words, the role of education should be to provide *models of coexistence* grounded on a rigorous intellectual approach, which 'draws on a rather exact notion of what it means to read philologically in a worldly and integrative mode and, at the same time, to offer resistance to the great reductive and vulgarising us-versus-them thought patterns of our time' (Said, 2004: 50). It should be possible for such models to replace those negative models of cultural exchange that silenced the professor in my vignette and in the process, deprived us all of the understanding he had of the changing nature of the society in which we now live.

Note

1   Can anybody assume this task? Does anyone have the faculty to speak truth to power? What does it mean to have a 'public role'? How does Said define the intellectual's audience?

References

Ali, T (2003) *The Clash of Fundamentalisms: crusades, jihads and modernity.* London: Verso

Anderson, B (1983) *Imagined Communities: reflections on the origin and spread of nationalism, 2nd edition.* London: Verso

Ashcroft, B and Ahluwalia, P (1999) *Edward Said.* London: Routledge

Benda, J (1980) *The Treason of the Intellectuals.* London: Norton

Bhabha, H (1994) *Location of Culture.* London: Routledge

Clifford, J (1980) Review of Orientalism. *History and Theory* 19(2) p204-223

Gramsci, A (1973) *The Prison Notebooks.* London; Lawrence and Wishart

Huntington, S (1996) *The Clash of Civilisations and Remaking of World Order.* New York: Simon and Shuster

Jayasuriya, K (2002) September 11, security, and the new postliberal politics of fear. In E Hershberg and KW Moore (eds) *Critical Views of September 11.* New York: The New Press

Lukes, S and Urbinati, N (2001) *Words Matter.* http://www.opendemocracy.net/forum/docu (accessed March 2007)

Said, E (1983) *The World, the Text and the Critic.* Cambridge, MA: Harvard University Press

Said, E (1993) *Culture and Imperialism.* New York: Knopf/Random House

Said, E. (1994a) *Culture and Imperialism.* New York: First Vintage Books

Said, E (1994b) *Representations of the Intellectual: 1993 Reith Lectures.* New York: Basic Books

Said, E (2001) Edward Said on Samuel Huntington. *Al Ahram Weekly On-line,* 11-17 October, No. 555

Said, E (2004) *Humanism and Democratic Criticism.* New York: Columbia University Press

Spivak, G (1987) Can the subaltern speak? In B Ashcroft, G Griffiths and H Tiffin (eds) *The Post-Colonial Studies Reader.* London: Routledge

Yuval-Davis, N (2001) The Binary War. http://www.opendemocracy.net/forum/docu (accessed May 2007)

9

Blaspheming Self-Image: the reinterpretation of African American identity and other disruptions of contemporary master narratives

JAMES HAYWOOD ROLLING, JR.

This work is an examination of the social construction of self and difference, and the discursive negotiation of master narratives of identity as an agency for change. It argues that a disruptive model of the interpretation of identity – blasphemies of given names, cultural stereotypes, and other symbols held sacred – can initiate incursions that reposition social power relations, as is evidenced in the reinterpretation of African American identity in the latter half of the twentieth century. This work of research is an unholy triptych of a sort, an affront to the methodolatry of objectivity, and is based on a trilogy originally published in *Qualitative Inquiry* exploring the intersection of autoethnography, critical race theory, and performance studies.

A more truthful quality of inquiry

In Jane Gooding-Brown's (2000) examination of the social construction of self and difference, and the negotiation of established interpretations as an agency for change, she argues that a disruptive model of interpretation can initiate incursions that reposition story values.

127

Agency is conceived here not as the 'freedom to do whatever the subject wills but rather freedom to constitute oneself in an unexpected manner-to decode and recode one's identity' (Stinson, 2004: 57). In the space of three recent autoethnographic writings revisited and condensed here, I have explored the kind of disruptions in discourse that can reposition the identity of a person or a people. At the start of these writings, I repositioned my identity in opposition to that of my father, master of his own high-walled obsidian city, hard and glassy to the touch. I desecrated his title as my sire by rewriting him, usurping the position he once claimed for himself when he often asserted that he knew me better than I knew myself. I also challenged the expectation of objectivity in research writing through the methodology of autoethnography, the sudden death of my father becoming the focal point but not the sole point of my research.

Autoethnography contends with proprieties both in social roles and acts of research, interrogating and thus disrupting the insistence of authoritative and abstract analyses, and allowing new interpretive stories to be insinuated into any discourse (Ellis and Bochner, 2006; Gooding-Brown, 2000). Mary Louise Pratt (1994) has defined an autoethnography as 'a text in which people undertake to describe themselves in ways that engage with representations others have made of them' (1994: 28).

Short biography

I contend that there is a relevancy worth pursuing in messing around with identity constructs in qualitative inquiry. The value of such pursuits is very much in keeping with the continuing emergence of '*the self as an instrument*' of qualitative studies (Eisner, 1991: 33, emphasis in the original). The purpose of such instruments is to augment objectivity, to arrive at a better quality and representation of acquired knowledge about our messy humanity, and to do so by messing around with the modernist master narratives that would constrain the indecorous splatter of our inquiry.

I was once asked to write a short biography of myself that was to be positioned to follow a book review that was eventually published in a prominent research journal. I was limited to a form of three sentences and it constitutes an example of a structuralist identity construct:

James Haywood Rolling, Jr. was once an ABD doctoral student in art education, and director of academic administration in the Department of Curriculum and Teaching at Teachers College, Columbia University, New York, USA. His research focused on poststructuralist interrogations of the certainties and norms of modernity, examining the archaeologies underlying the (re)constitution of social identities from previous interpretations ensconced in visual culture. He was the editorial assistant of the research journal *Studies in Art Education* and once served as an adjunct faculty at New York University, USA.

Structuralism is a science of structures, a deterministic meta-structure of modern assumptions suggesting how what have together been identified as the principal elements of language, literature and culture network together to make us who we purportedly are. Autoethnography is a practice that moves into the foreground 'the multiple nature of selfhood and opens up new ways of writing about social life' (Reed-Danahay, 1997: 3). It is a methodology that questions the authenticity of the voice that tells of an essential self.

Obituary

I have very specific early bodily/spatial memories of my father – it usually involved being hit, slapped, poked, prodded, spanked or stood up against a wall and lectured to at length, *ad nauseam*. Never hugging, never holding hands, never a piggyback ride, never a pat on the shoulder declaiming, 'Well done, my good boy'. This essential self I knew was the insecurity of a child who knew he wasn't good enough to live up to the name. Writing his obituary after his sudden death, I asserted my own power to reconstitute his dead body. I assembled the evidence that he once lived from fragments of his life, my memory, an old résumé, found letters, his job newsletters, newspaper articles, conversations with family and his friends, his grandmother's obituary, his mother's obituary and her final letter to her only child – carefully kept in a blue envelope for over 35 years, written on browning blue stationery. Each 'fact' was drawn into proximity from a different angle of repose to author an interpretation that suited my purposes.

As the last surviving James Haywood Rolling, my name is itself constituted of subliminal self-images posing me in many specific situations against the larger, more formidable, more threatening, more unpredictable elder Rolling. A poststructural identity construct takes me a step further towards an unfettered freedom to un-name names and to name myself, a self-concept unbounded from authorial pens and validating structures. Recovering from loss has pushed me forward to a place that 'lies ahead, in the unfolding of the story, not behind waiting to be regained' (Warner, 1995: 111). Counter-intuitively, a new home is regained in the descent into chaos and loss. In order to further mess up my normal constructs and tell of new poststructural possibilities – to restore the agency that allows me to disembowel a discourse of sublimation rather than be disembodied and delimited by it – I turn now to Laurel Richardson. Richardson (1997: 143) describes the 'poetic representation of lives' as that which 'reveals the process of self-construction, the reflexive basis of self-knowledge, the inconsistencies and contradictions of a life spoken as a meaningful whole' by a poem that has the simultaneous quality of acting as a whole to make sense of its parts, while as a whole it can be experienced through its parts or subtexts.

The poetics of self-image

Self-image is self-naming. Our self-images are variations in an ongoing and embodied and personal story; thus, they are malleable. Self-image, like memory, can be erased by time or modified as facts, are forgotten or misremembered over time. Self-image can be contorted by falsehoods or accusations. Self-image can be invaded by trauma or brain lesion. Self-image can be altogether disconnected from factuality and be reinforced by fictional episodes or fantasies. Self-image can be recalled by alternative cues, and be remembered in emotional keys varying from the discordant to the melodious. An individual's archaeology of self-imagery is a story-in-progress. This story is intuitively told, proceeding 'from everything we know and everything we are'; this story is improvised and, as with all improvisations, converges 'on the moment from a rich plurality of directions and sources' (Nachmanovitch, 1990: 40). The human facility to shape divergent variations of truth around facts that remain the same makes any name, label, or category highly contestable.

How then does the un-named body re/figure itself out? How do I root myself in an alternative self-image? How does the new name – the un-inherited legacy, the nonessentialist caregiver – become home, a new and researchable framework for identity? How do I tell myself to others as a professor of worth, an owner of valuable intellectual property, rather than as an orphan? As an African American, my perspective on the necessity of un-naming and re-naming has been engendered as a result of the history of Western social practices of image-making. By interrupting 'the monolithic assumptions and metanarratives of modernism' with irony and the indeterminate signs as the change agents toward a reconstituted self, art historian Michael D. Harris (2003: 20) suggests the 'possibility that blacks formed the first postmodern population at the beginning of modernism'.

As a social being, I have been ferociously and visually named – Bad, Bad Leroy Brown, the brutal black buck; Topsy or Buckwheat, the untamed, unkempt, watermelon-eating picanniny; Uncle Tom, the smiling, wide-eyed, docile servant; Aunt Jemima, the obese, utterly contented, pitch black maternal figure; Jezebel, the uninhibited whore, fulfiller of all sexual fantasies; Sambo, the lazy, inarticulate buffoon; Jim Crow or Zip Coon, the travelling darkie entertainers, song-and-dance minstrels; Peola, the quadroon, the self-hating mulatto, poisoned with the scourge of Negro blood and the selfishness of white social aspirations; Golliwog, the grotesque and alien rag doll, the antithesis of porcelain beauty.

Can identity be created from the reinterpretation of identity? The visual representation of the African American body in Western visual culture has been unique in the all-out effort of those who sought to define us as either less than human, less than American, less than Christian or less than statistically significant. Represented in this fashion, our bodies became enclaves for the agency of Western hegemony; we became a part of the discourse of modernity, not entirely whole unless we were in obeisance to the title story. Conversely, when we developed responses, indigenous and idiosyncratic responses, our responses entered the discourses of public opinion and modern popular culture and resonated there, changing meaning. It is not primarily through the sciences but through the arts that our names, labels, categories and stereotypes may be rethought and overwritten – broken down into their innumerable possibilities.

Junior

The consideration of how we are 'to rethink ourselves' (Bhabha, 1994: 65) is dangerous to the sustainability of the state and *status quo*, to the permanence of a tainting authority. To rethink self is to un-name self, to un-ink, to un-stick self. To un-name self is to blaspheme the origin of the name; to un-name self is to unravel threads of nomenclatural heresy in a denouement of the lineage of the dictatorial meme.

My father wanted me to be just like him, or an extension of him, or the as yet unrealised possibility of him, hence the replication of his name in full on my birth certificate, with the minor appellation of Junior to contextualise me. He called himself 'Jim' so I was nick-named 'Jim-Jim' and each time I was so called, I was indeed nicked. I was the determinable scion. My father often said, 'I know you better than you know yourself'. Nicked again in spirit, diminished in independence, I always bled when he repeated this. He did not know my friends, my loves, my failures, my aspirations, the intimate places I had discovered on my body; therefore, he did not know me. Of course, I was afraid to tell him this directly. My body was smaller than his and, while growing up, I was used to the unexpected flash of his hard hand to my belly or head when I had committed some unknowable offence to his unwavering common sense. I was no stranger to being doubled over in pain; I was accustomed to being struck dizzy. One day he became aware that I had developed an automatic response, a duck of the head, a bob, a weave, a twist of the body when his hand moved unexpectedly within my peripheral sight – even if he was just reaching for a cup from the dish rack. He stopped striking me so often, which had the strangely adverse effect of diminishing our physical contact in the home.

My father, an artist, did a portrait of me when I was a child, although it was never given to me while I was still a child. That portrait, in a white file drawer for most of my life until it was revisited at some point in the last years of his life, was finally given to me soon before he died. My hair, originally painted solid black, was revised for reasons never expressed to me. In its place, something rhizomatic is indicated. Perhaps it is a reference to the insufferable difference between his expectations for his firstborn son and my wilfulness in navigating my own identity through life's curricular spaces. Perhaps it is a relenting, an acknowledgement of the failure of his first draft of my biography.

But my father also attempted an autobiography. I found it in the form of an unfinished children's picture book as I was filtering through his studio after his death in 2002. I was re-searching, trying to make sense of this man, of my intent to blaspheme, of my irreverent effort to transpose subservience and agency within the delimiting space of my given names. In taking a distinctly autobiographical stance to the writing of this research, I am in accord with Michael Humphreys in his intent 'to interweave an autoethnographic ... story with methodological theory and to 'draw an audience into a collective experience in which a version of truth is demonstrated for the collective to judge" (Humphreys 2005: 855, citing Butler, 1997). Sociologist Laurel Richardson (1997: 32) describes 'a collective story' as that which gives voice to those marginalised or silenced, to those sired and sociologically constructed either in the house where I grew up in Crown Heights, Brooklyn, or in the prevailing western enlightenment and hegemonic narrative where I have also grown up. I give voice to myself. I give voice to the collective.

Precursor

It turns out that I am actually James Haywood Rolling, III. I found a letter my father wrote of his family lineage from his grandmother Eva, as legally required for a property settlement about six months after her death on January 11, 1983. He writes:

> Eva Haywood [Rolling] had one other son, James Haywood Rolling. He and his wife, Eva (Hart) Rolling had one child, me, James H. Rolling Jr. My father, James senior, died when I was very young and my mother passed away in 1965. I reside at 1260 Lincoln Place, Brooklyn, N.Y. 11213. (James Haywood Rolling, Jr., personal communication, July 13, 1983)

To un-name is to undermine purported origins, to burrow between the archaeologies that constrain, to initiate and inaugurate anomalous genealogies that thrive and proliferate and die and leach new life between the layers. To un-name is to give light to discursive ephemeralities that may live for just a day, but whose names are no less alive, no less legitimate in quality than the vast tectonic ecologies of foundational and constrictive archaeologies. My own autobiography interacts with particular archaeologies – archaeologies in this case defined as the multiformational arrangement of positions in the discourse of fathers and their relationships with their sons – as perpetuated in the autobiography of the familial sire, the narrative that was found in my eulogised father's art studio. My autobiography also interacts with the multiformational arrangement of positions in the discourse of Western forefathers and their relationships with their human capital, their investment progeny – as perpetuated in the autobiography of the hegemonic sire, the narrative that is found in the messy tracts of race negotiation in the United States.

Both narratives have been conserved for my hand to overwrite, to un-name. In this overwriting, the first narrative – one of my father's narratives – is framed as a children's story, yet works simultaneously to hide and reveal a lifetime of discontent. The second narrative – one of my forefathers' narratives – was formed into the comic song 'Ten Little Indians' in 1868 by Philadelphia songwriter Septimus Winner. Reframed as the nursery rhyme and popular children's song 'Ten Little Niggers' in 1939 by Frank Green, it perpetuates an outright erasure of the value of little Black boys who might grow up to be Black men. Writing between the lines and pages of both my father and foster forefathers, I have insinuated elements of my autobiography within both the recollections of my father's childhood, and my nation's ode to the Manifest Destiny of the spectators of ten scripted lynchings:

Big brown mama ain't what she used to be. She's changed. Doesn't love me anymore. Rearranged. Dancing. Prancing. No more romancing.

> My tall brown grandma, barely remembered
> dying behind embroidered curtains
> away from light and child's-eye view
> lung cancer ate her
> before I was two
> I did not know he loved her so
> I did not know she hurt him so
> loving an abusive boyfriend more than her only son.

> Ten little nigger boys went out to dine.

Hey cityboy, it's easy to have fun. Stay out of the sun. Carry a gun. Drugs for sale. Learn to run.

> Cityboy writing himself incompletely,
> sire of the last James Haywood Rolling,

raised without his greater James Haywood Rolling,
a tubercular trumpet player gone by twenty-one;
leaving little Brownsville cityboy, having some kinds of fun
avoiding the guns, the kindling urban sun
running small-time numbers, outrunning big-time drugs.

One choked his little self, and then there were nine.

Gram taught me a lot. How to read. What to put in a pot. Respect
your brother and every body's mother.

Eva, mother of my father's dead father,
outlived Little Eva, my father's mother,
outlived Uncle Elmo, her own one-eyed son
until she died downstairs on the musty first floor
of 1260 Lincoln Place, the house we grew up in,
Gram's home, passed on to my father,
my father's house, not ours.

Nine little nigger boys sat up very late.

Start a new job, can't bask in the sun. Working's no fun. There won't
be a loss, just impress the boss.

Stubbornly an artist
while other colored men sought jobs
with pensions and pay grades,
he toiled at J. C. Penney's product displays
for too little pay,
a former army illustrator and his first son on the way.

One overslept himself, and then there were eight.

Ma loved me, and gave me full support. She hurried and scurried,
worked and praised, and worried until I was raised.

Rising at the end of cityboyhood
was there finally a return of the love
so long deprived
administered in her helpless attentions
as he in turn nursed her into oblivion?

Eight little nigger boys travelling in Devon.

My wife, Syl, a wonderful gal. Loving, silly, what a pal. We raised
four kids, that was tough. Results ... good enough.

135

Wasn't Ma wife enough to also put her name on the lease?
Couldn't four kids meet the measure of your trust
to have a single friend over when you were not home?
Did I ever evolve beyond a mere 'bird brain,' as you put it,
develop enough warrant to be called by your name?

One said he'd stay there, and then there were seven.

My wife bought a car, now it's her turn. Insurance. Repair. Bills.
Scratches. Dents. Parking. She pays out. Now she'll care.

Always teaching lessons to your wife
To all the lesser beings in your life
To the lesser minds, the lesser bodies
that disturbed your reign of common sense.

Seven little nigger boys chopping up sticks.

Used to be nice. Don't think twice. Walk day or night. Nice neigh-
bours. Lots of ice cream flavours. Gone forever.

I try to remember the ice cream parlours you took us to.
Sometimes you did, you would say.
I wish I remembered it so every day.
We were so young when you took us to the circus,
or smuggled us in to Saturday movie matinees,
at the price of kids younger than we were
until we grew up and spoiled all our fun.

One chopped himself in half, and then there were six.

Cheapest, best game in town. Hit the ball against the wall. Who's the
champ? Beat the rest. The best player wins.

Didn't you know I played handball too?
How come you never came to see one of my games?
I played them right here under the tall white turrets
of the urine-stained schoolyard walls.

Six little nigger boys playing with a hive.

Use a paddle. Don't hurt your hand. Hit the ball hard. Put your name
on the card. Four on. Winners next.

I remember you inviting me once to play,
but you were more interested in winning that day
than in helping me develop my game.
Did you know I used to beat men old enough to be my father?

Did you know that your paddleball trophies are in a box I carried
with me to Happy Valley, PA?

A bumble-bee stung one, and then there were five.

City folks on a picnic. A long drive. Music. Jive. Fun to survive. Tough
days ahead. Fall. Winter. Enjoy the good times.

High flaming barbecues on steel and concrete public grills;
family outings to the Long Island state park
eating my Ma's potato salad
and Aunt Ernestine's fried chicken
from Tupperware bins,
Koolaid dripping in the grass from the broken thermos spout
inciting bees to drunken violence.

Five little nigger boys going in for law.

City children. Grow up fast. Or you don't last. Drugs. Bugs. Rats.
Mice. Lice. Get a job. Raise a family. Nice!

Raising a family of six on an art director's salary,
your insecurity must have overwhelmed you,
whenever you shielded the combination
to the safe in your dark closet
from strangers you kept inside your home,
peeking over your wide shoulders for some demonstration of love.
I never really knew that man at the end of his life
hoarding lottery tickets organised in white plastic grocery bags
discovered as we emptied the house from room to room.
Thousands of dollars that failed to yield that storied payout
that Gram first used to buy the house on Lincoln Place.

One got in chancery, and then there were four.

Pray for us, through the times we've had, good and bad. Sad. Be glad.
Deliver us from evil. Thy kingdom comes.

People hand in hand
I'm not one who make believes
Today's not yesterday
And all things have an ending
Could a place like this exist so beautiful
Or were the friendly neighbours of old Crown Heights
just an inner vision of Stevie Wonder's mind?

Four little nigger boys going out to sea.

Our dog. Home alone. Family at work ... school. Coco was her name.
Chewing furniture was her game. No more loco Coco.

> I could not bear the inapplicability of the name;
> my second uttered blasphemy was told
> when the family decided they would call the new dog Coco,
> and I decided to call her Sandy,
> calling her by her color, or not at all.
> Sandy's senses shattered slowly over three years,
> from too many firecrackers, too many sharp noises in overly sensitive ears
> until we put her out of her misery and out of our minds.

> A red herring swallowed one, and then there were three.

We played. We stayed. Together. Fun. Sun. Study buddy. Old friends
yesterday. Court. Marry. Divorce. Don't speak to each other today.

> Our godfathers disappeared one by one,
> after each fallout with their buddy, Jim.
> My father had a way of drawing lines
> and in spite of the changes in people or time,
> retracing those lines daily on the ground
> in an array of colored chalks.

> Three little nigger boys walking in the zoo.

Tough games on the handball court. Killer Ron. Roadrunner Mel.
Play all day. Who doesn't give up? Mel wins going away.

> But you left the chess out of the story, Da...!
> (I could never bring myself to affectionately utter 'Dad')
> Men came to your funeral
> who played chess in the park with you for fifteen years,
> men who did not know your given name
> men the family never knew,
> men who knew only the nickname they awarded you
> warranted by the style and strength of your game,
> men who mourned and said they called you 'Nemesis'.

> A big bear hugged one, and then there were two.

Delancey Street. Street vendors. Push carts. Stops and starts. Sale.
Everything. From rugs to kale. Fast. Can't last. Start again tomorrow.

> The loss of the local block association in which you served
> to the pace of the city, the pace of the sameness,

the loss of the street to anonymous neighbours,
to six-foot outdoor speakers rattling beats all night
against our neighbours' windows,
the loss of your family to misdeeds and mistrust.
It could not have escaped your attention
that once the kids grow up and flee the house,
once Ma leaves to buy a co-op in her name,
it's too late to start again.

Two little nigger boys sitting in the sun.

Play your numbers. Argue. Fight. Bars. Pimps. Hang out. All night.
Ghetto children. What a life. Living ... existing on Fulton Street.

Was this a children's book you ever planned to sell?
Was this a cautionary tale? Was this your way of reaching the
lost?
Like you did at the Harlem youth centre,
doing public penance for a lifetime of reserve?

One got frizzled up, and then there was one.

Gram's brother. Uncle Ed. Minister. Brownsville's biggest church.
Take advantage of family. Friends. Saint Paul's the start. Bay Shore's
the end.

The scars must have been deeper than anyone knew
What did Uncle Ed do to you
that forever kept you from wooden pews?

One little nigger boy living all alone.

Target practice. Drugs. Innocent people hit. Caught in the middle.
Bad guys unharmed. Couldn't hit the side of a burning barn.

I watched you fall half asleep on the couch
I watched you fall asleep half awake
I saw the fear of facing the sum of your life
'Was I one of the bad guys?' I heard you ask
as the TV blared in the a.m. hours
while the radio droned at the highest volume
until your voice that final day home alone
could no longer be raised at anyone.

He got married, and then there were none.

I am the last James Haywood Rolling. Perhaps, as written by Western hegemony, all Black men are lost boys destroyed by discourse, each a Junior, a minor appellation, a given name, a little nigger, awaiting their role in the quantitative countdown, the call to perform the existential escape clause, to self-correct the mistake of being born Black. Perhaps all Black men are James Haywood Rolling, Jr., just as my father and I have been. Perhaps my father, who always signed his name Jim Rolling, was the strong one, long ago overthrowing his patriarchal sires, never adhering to the name James Haywood Rolling, Jr. Or perhaps my father was the weak one, succumbing to cumulative incapability of producing all that he had desired, including a firstborn son who was just like him – these were not inabilities stemming from lack of desire, but perhaps for lack of desire for an un-named life. In this research, I act to un-name all other Juniors in the act of un-naming myself. Those unborn. Those postmortem. Those unfathered. This is, after all, a collective story.

This is a collaboration that conspires not to wholly vanquish conquerors but to coexist and supplant, James itself being a name of Biblical derivation, meaning 'supplanter', or to supersede and replace. As I write and breathe, all previous Jameses recede from the page, all preceding monsters and myths withdraw from history, and I am left dripping in the thaw of the delimiting text. In supplanting, I accept a new agency, that of a secular blasphemer. I gladly do so. Secular blasphemy is 'a transgressive act of cultural translation', translation being 'the performative nature of cultural communication' consisting of [the principle and practice of the] movement of meaning' (Bhabha 1994: 226-228). There is no ultimate end to translational and transposing communication, as it 'puts the original in motion to decanonise it, giving it the movement of fragmentation, a wandering of errance, a kind of permanent exile (de Man, 1986: 92). There is no personal agenda except that in my journey through exile, I have become possible once again.

Implications to power

As seen in the failed foreign policy of our modern presidential namesake to flex his muscles and shove American-styled democracy in the face of Iraqi people, paradigms of personal and social identity, unlike political regimes, do not crumble from without except by a slow erosion and they do not topple suddenly from their internal foundations except by an earthquake from within. More importantly, whether by erosion from without or by a quaking from within, fundamental (or fundamentalist) public policy approaches at home or abroad will only alter if the paradigm of identity that organises them is first decanonised.

The unspoken brilliance of the United States Civil Rights movement in the 1960s was not that it directly rewrote public policies, but that it effectively shook up long-standing paradigms of identity in the republic. Prior to the real-time theatre of Civil Rights demonstrations, the majority of the American public actually believed that African Americans were content with their meagre lot and with invisibility as stakeholders in the American dream. African Americans had kept and had been kept silent about their unrest for so long, it was genuinely shocking for White Americans to see Black Americans in their living rooms on television, publicly risking and sacrificing their lives in the demonstration of deeply felt and apparently long-held discontent. When the equally long-held paradigm of the 'happy, carefree Negro' was shattered, public policies enforcing segregation and disenfranchisement also began to fall by the wayside with astonishing speed.

To cut their losses in this very public deconstruction of self-image and identity, politicians, officials and activists, often with very different agendas, were all similarly motivated to mitigate the waves of disruption buffeting the psyches and the categories of the communities of those they represented, waves redistributing the powers that held the *status quo* – waves decanonising the power of secular names held sacred with truth that was in the making. Concessions and compromises were ultimately made. Politics quelled the visible movement. However, beneath the surface of contemporary complacencies of self-image in the new century, new truths are still moving and reshaping the public geography. The ongoing poststructural slippage of previous demographic demarcations has called public identity into question worldwide, with mandated ID cards a new form of reactionary structuralism (Privacy International, 2004). Notwithstanding the desperation of the conservative, or the desperation of those travelling in exile, public paradigms of self-image and identity, no matter how entrenched they may seem, are bound to be un-named with the birth of the next supplanter.

References

Bhabha, H (1994) *The Location of Culture.* London and New York: Routledge

Butler, R (1997) Stories and experiments in social inquiry. *Organization Studies* 18(6) p927-948

de Man, P (1986) *The Resistance to Theory (Theory and History of Literature, Volume 33).* Minneapolis: University of Minnesota Press

Eisner, E (1991) *The Enlightened Eye: qualitative inquiry and the enhancement of educational practice.* New York: Macmillan

Ellis, C and Bochner, A (2006) Analyzing Analytic Ethnography: an autopsy. *Journal of Contemporary Ethnography* 35(4) p429-449

Gooding-Brown, J (2000) Conversations About Art: a disruptive model of interpretation. *Studies in Art Education* 42(1) p36-50

Harris, M (2003) *Colored Pictures: race and visual representation.* Chapel Hill: The University of North Carolina Press

Humphreys, M (2005) Getting Personal: reflexivity and autoethnographic vignettes. *Qualitative Inquiry* 11(6) p840-860

Nachmanovitch, S (1990) *Free Play: the power of improvisation in life and the arts.* New York: Tarcher/Putnam Books

Pratt, M (1994) Transculturation and autoethnography: Peru 1615/1990. In F Barker, P Holme and M Iverson (eds) *Colonial Discourse/Postcolonial theory.* Manchester and New York: Manchester University Press

Reed-Danahay, D (ed) (1997) *Auto/Ethnography: rewriting the self and the social.* Oxford: Berg

Privacy International (2004) UK ID Card moving forward despite significant opposition. http://www.privacyinternational.org/article.shtml?cmd%5B347%5D=x-347-79542 (accessed December 2004)

Richardson, L (1997) *Fields of Play: constructing an academic life.* New Jersey: Rutgers University Press

Stinson, D (2004) African American male students and achievement in school mathematics: a critical postmodern analysis of agency. Unpublished doctoral dissertation, Georgia State University

Warner, M (1995) *Six Myths of Our Time: little angels, little monsters, beautiful beasts, and more.* New York: Vintage Books

10

The 'R' Word: voicing race as a critical problem and not just a problem of practice

PAUL WARMINGTON

Introduction

The welcome deconstruction of race and its claims to theoretical intelligibility has left us buckling under the weight of scare quotes, prefixes, suffixes, qualifiers and euphemisms. Today in academic papers, policy documents or classroom resources the word 'race' is frequently accompanied by inverted commas. In this context, in which the R word is so often circumvented, how can we speak not just of racism or racialisation but of race itself in the work that we do in classrooms? This chapter addresses some of the challenges of delineating race as a conceptual problem in higher education (HE) classrooms. It takes a counter-intuitive position: at least, for someone like me, a black academic who has taught around race equality issues on and off for almost twenty years in further and higher education. It queries the pedagogic comfort zone in which race is explicated as a social construct on the grounds that the social construct position, which I take to be correct in general, carries with it a tendency to depict race as a form of false consciousness destined for the dustbin of ideological illusions.

The chapter is concerned with how to focus in classrooms on race as a central social practice: something central to the social and political formation, not something that happens elsewhere and to other people. This is not to assume that race is the master factor in lived experience but rather to emphasise its non-aberrant, everyday quality. This chapter reflects on ways in which the problem of race is routinely opened up or shut down in classroom explorations. It considers the black-boxing of race, the limits of depicting race as illusory and the raced nature of notions such as culture and ethnicity. In conclusion, it begins to explore the possibility of using the concepts of boundary construction and pulsation as tools for thinking about the 'continuing significance and changing meaning of race' (Winant, 2000: 182).

Race, centrality and aberrance

This chapter, which draws in part on reflections upon my own teaching, qualifies the idea of race as a social construct in a number of ways. Firstly, it incorporates the highly contested terms 'race' and 'centrality'. The postmodern attachment to all things de-centred means that any claims about the centrality of race may raise reservations among some. On the other hand, conventional Marxist thinking on the centrality of social class and the epiphenomenal place of race (Miles, 1989, may be considered emblematic) may encourage a different brand of suspicion. The notion of centrality is used here modestly but as a necessary condition for embedding race as a conceptual problem in classrooms; it refers back to Gilroy's (1987: 148) key distinction between antiracist and anti-fascist activism, wherein he cautions that exaggerating the importance of far right groups in the definition of racism: 'risks the suggestion that racism is an aberration or an exceptional problem essentially unintegrated into the social and political structure'.

Thus the term centrality is voiced in opposition to the depiction of racism as an aberrant practice and of race as something that is lived only by others, something that remains exotic. As Gillborn (2005: 485) asserts, racism is 'a multifaceted, deeply embedded, often taken for granted aspect of power relations'. One *may* encounter BNP activity, one may experience the brick through the window or unlawful arrest but we will *certainly* encounter the raced, and sometimes racist, practices of school, college, health care, housing, the labour market and the media. The concern of this chapter is with race as an everyday doing, claiming and being done to. In classroom debates whether these raced practices result in damaging racist consequences may, at times, be bracketed; the initial learning step is the recognition of how and where race is played out through the deployment of raced boundaries, tools and categories. In short, racism is regarded in this chapter as a variant of doing race; clearly, doing race is a necessary condition for racist practices.

In opting to use the word 'race', as well as, where appropriate, 'racism' and 'racialisation', this chapter stresses verb-like and adjectival qualities, as well as the noun. Where Gilroy (1987) emphasises the normal, non-aberrant nature of racism, this chapter stresses also the normal, non-aberrant, non-exotic nature of raced practices: that is, the doing of race and the being done to. Race may lack theoretical or scientific integrity but it is a lived experience. Individuals in society, in practice live in ways that are informed by raced categories, inequalities and modes of distribution. We live with race as if it has meaning and we live within a society in which those raced meanings have innumerable consequences. We live with race as a social fact. As Winant (2000: 184) insists:

> The longevity of the race concept and the enormous number of effects of race thinking (and race acting) has produced a guarantee that race will remain a feature of social reality across the globe ... at the level of experience of everyday life; race is a relatively impermeable part of our identity ... To be raceless is akin to being genderless.

In learning and teaching in Higher Education, an understanding that society is sinewed by raced practices is necessary to critical consideration of the nature of racism and particular instances of racism. Without this understanding, racism is exoticised and, when confronted with questions of whether a particular practice or instance is racist, some students are inevitably left asking, 'How could this instance have moved from normality to something as aberrant, as exotic as racism? Surely that sort of thing doesn't happen here'.

The idea that race is a mediating tool and that social relationships are mediated by race is important in this chapter. The concept of race as a tool (or cultural artefact) is informed by sociocultural theories of mediation, wherein societies, groups and individuals alter the world through the production and appropriation of cultural artefacts and are themselves altered by developing and using those artefacts. It may offer a way beyond debates about the supposed reification of race: debates as to whether race takes on a life of its own, beyond supposedly more real, determining social and economic relationships (Hall, 1980; Miles, 1989). For the moment, it may at least be a way of taking race outside the realm of illusion, of scare quotes. Race may not be a real biological category; however, it has reality as a mediating tool, a social artefact. This chapter does not allow for an extensive discussion of cultural mediation.

With regard to work on race in the UK, however, in its Althusserian anti-reductionist reading of Marx, Hall's (1980) seminal *Race, Articulation and Societies Structured in Dominance* provided a key challenge to those concerned with theorising race in terms of its articulation with social class – that is, class as relationship to mode of production. In short, Hall (1980) set out to retain several key Marxist concepts but argued that while the economic level is a necessary condition for explaining race as a political-ideological function, it is not a sufficient condition for explanation. Hall's (1980) early explorations of the dynamics in race theorisation between an economic tendency that is analytical, or 'explanatory', but simplificatory, and a sociological tendency that is rich and complex but descriptive, find echoes in subsequent spats between, for instance Gilroy (1987, 1993) and Miles (1984; 1989) and, in the USA, between Winant (2000) and Fields (1990; 2003). All of these complex positions and oppositions are concerned with mediation in that they theorise race from historicist perspectives but contest notions of agency, relative autonomy, reification and explanation. In extremely crude terms, their writings stake a series of competing positions on the old questions of (i) whether race takes on a life of its own, relatively autonomous of relations of production, and (ii) whether it is valid in a world of mediations to ask the first question.

Race as a conceptual problem in classrooms

What does it mean to point to race as a conceptual problem in the classroom? I have reflected on my lesson plans, presentation slides and post-session field notes from undergraduate and taught postgraduate sessions over the past two years, as well as reflecting on subject meetings and informal discussions with staff teaching around race in my own and other institutions. As a lecturer in Higher Education, my main input in Education Studies programmes has been into undergraduate programmes, from which many of the students will progress either to PGCE courses, or else teaching and supervising on postgraduate programmes, in which the majority of students are experienced education professionals. As I teach in one of England's most culturally diverse cities, the groups are ethnically mixed. In undergraduate sessions almost all students are home students. My estimate[1] is that 65 – 75% of student participants are white (this conflates white British, Irish and minority white ethnic groups) and that the remaining 25 – 35% students are mainly Indian, Pakistani, African, African-Caribbean, Chinese or mixed race. In undergraduate groups the proportion of white students tends to be slightly larger and there are, I would estimate, slightly more overseas students.

The themes of my sessions, broadly described, have focused on patterns of inequality around race and ethnicity, on conceptualising race and on researching into issues of race equality and education. Among the aims of the sessions, which are made explicit to the student groups, are:

- developing understanding of the historicity of the concept of race

- developing understanding of race as a social construct

- working with dynamic, relational meanings of race and interrogating essentialism

- reflecting on raced practices (the production of racialised boundaries and the content of racialised categories)

- examining the intersection of race and other differences and inequalities

- reflecting upon the difficulties posed in developing tools for analysing and critiquing race and its effects.

The minimal learning aim in these classes might be defined simply as the recognition that race is a conceptual problem; in other words, there are conceptual (and therefore, methodological, political and ethical) problems created by the everyday usage of race as a category and by the everyday usage of race's current myriad related categories and sub-categories: such as Asian, African-Caribbean, black, white, asylum seeker, Muslim women.

Opening up race's black-box

In considering mediation and historical agency, Latour (1999) offers an illuminating take on subject-tool-object relationships. For Latour action is not simply the property of human subjects but of complex networks or assemblages of people, concepts, tools and technologies. In everyday practices, complex assemblages are often 'black-boxed': that is, regarded as single entities. Often it is not until the settlement on which the assemblage depends breaks down, that the black-box is opened up to reveal its constituent parts (Law, 1992). A college, for example, is a complex assemblage of workers, concepts and technologies. The assemblage is not revealed in the statement, 'I'm going to college today'; however, the black-box is opened up if one is put in the position of having to say, 'I'm not going to college today because the lab has flooded and Sheila hasn't found plumbers to fix it'. In such an instance the relational components of the assemblage that comprises the college are disassembled.

In a classroom session exploring race it might be argued that shifts in learning are enabled by pointing to race as a problem space and finding ways to prompt the opening up of the black-box that is race. A technique I have used repeatedly is to open classes simply by grouping students and asking them the question, 'what is race?' Frequent responses have been:

- it's something to do with physical appearance
- it's something to do with ethnicity, culture, religion, language and nationality
- it's something to do with physical appearance but also ethnicity, culture, etc.
- it's a commonly used idea but it's difficult to explain

This range of overlapping responses draws attention to residual notions of race as a somatic referent but also to social construct notions of race as encompassing intersections between somatic distinctions and cultural differentiation.

The 'what is race' question is useful because it tends, at the very least, to produce a default consensus as to the *unintelligibility* of the concept of race, hence the oft-used construction, which I've appropriated above, 'It's something to do with ...'. It encourages the beginnings of a shift away from everyday meanings and uses of race because it provides a simple instance of the concept of race *not* working. It is an initial opening up of race's black-box. This problematisation of race can be seen when, as happened in one of my recent undergraduate sessions, a white student responded to the 'what is race?' question by answering on behalf of his small discussion group: 'It's hard to explain what race is but you know what it means when you're using it'. This was an acknowledgment of the gap between everyday contingencies and ontological meaning. The session went on to focus, in large part, on the historical development of race as a social category and the unstable nature of its sub-categories and boundaries, with reference to issues such as equal opportunities monitoring.

Race: what it is not

Such reverse black-boxing also offers the opportunity for discussion of what race is not. As Ladson-Billings (1998) and Omi and Winant (1986) argue, the dominant focus of anti-racist teaching has been critiquing race as natural, as biologistic. Integral to this critical project, which has been mapped out in the broad contours drawn by Dubois, Fanon and Said, is the location of race as a historically specific phenomenon. Such critiques draw upon analyses of the processes and legacies of imperialism, the discursive production of race and the role of racialisation in sustaining labour divisions and hierarchies. Needless to say, this thumbnail sketch cannot do justice to the nuances of the vast body of historical analyses of the concept of race, in which there are heterogeneous takes on areas such as relationships between the labour process and the political-ideological sphere (Hall, 1980; Sivanandan, 1982; Delgado 2003; Cole, 2004, 2008); the roles of representation, identity and mediation (hooks, 1990; Gilroy 1993, 2005; Goldberg, 1993, Bhabha, 1994); intersections between race, gender and other formations of lived experience (Davis, 1982; Collins, 1990; Delgado and Stefancic, 2000).

However, a gloss on the historicisation of race, wherein its genealogy and its function as artefact are opened up historically, might include the following strands. The notion of race is a modern invention, the roots of which lie in the justifications of the plantation economy and in the pseudo-sciences of the eighteenth and nineteenth centuries. These pseudo-sciences codified relatively scrappy myths about cultural and physical difference into a systematic categorisation of human beings into distinct 'bio-cultural' types. The key features of the concept of race were that human types were distinguished by absolute and permanent bio-genetic and cultural differences. These supposedly fixed differences were held to indicate a permanent hierarchy of racial superiority and inferiority (Fryer, 1988; Cole, 2004). Pseudo-scientific notions of race have long been discredited in mainstream scientific and political thought – although they resurface periodically, not least in Anglo-American academia. Consequently, the notion of race is one with which many of us, rightly, feel uneasy. It should also be stressed that, while racism has been integral to modernity, the struggle against racism has also been central to the development of modernity.

However, the continued belief in essentialist models of race and discrete racial or ethnic identities may not always draw upon a pseudo-scientific warrant. References to Muslims since 2001 as a culturally distinct, homogenous grouping are but one example of the racialisation of culture and ethnicity (Kundnani, 2007). This does not refer simply to the association of Islam with, say, Pakistani or Bangladeshi people but to the notion of permanent, impermeable boundaries between cultures. In this discourse, culture becomes the fixed indicator of the dispositions of individuals and whole communities and signifies supposedly fixed differences, just as surely as pseudo-scientific racial phenotypes once did. My point here is that while the treacherous quality of the word race is nowadays widely acknowledged, terms such as ethnicity, culture and diversity, which are often suggested as preferable alternatives, are also loaded and should also be interrogated in classrooms.

Elsewhereing race

In taught sessions the foregrounding of race as a social practice offers space to students to reflect upon raced experiences. It can enable subsequent discussion about raced experiences of education, health, housing and employment, indicating difference, diversity and social inequalities in a way that emphasises race as a process of historical and social organisation with different consequences for different people but without drifting into essentialism. However, Winant (2000) has cautioned against taking complacent refuge in the notion of race as a social construct – or, rather, as an ideological construct. His core criticism is that, in regarding race as an ideological construct, a kind of false consciousness, we run the risk of underestimating 'the salience a social construct can develop over half a millennium or more of diffusion ... as a fundamental principle of social organisation and identity formation' (*ibid*: 184).

Winant (2000) critiques Fields (1990), who takes a position similar to Young (2006) and Miles (1989), for seeking to explain race and racism as barely mediated expressions of the economic base. Winant acknowledges that Fields contributes to the understanding of the origins of raced thinking in the American context. However, her 'assertion that race is an ideological construct – understood in the sense of a 'false consciousness' that explains other 'material relations' in distorted fashion' is, argues Winant, extremely problematic, based as it seemingly is on the unsupportable dichotomy that since race is not an objective scientific fact it can only be 'an illusion that does ideological work' (Winant, 2000: 183). Fields (1990: 118) also presents a temporal dichotomy between the past of American slavery and immediate post-emancipation when, she argues, the ideological function of the concept of race served a clear economic logic and a *present*, in which race is kept artificially alive by representational drives that 'create and recreate it in our social lives (and) continue to verify it'. In arguing for this dichotomy, Fields (1990, 2003), like Young (2006), locates race as happening 'elsewhere': in this case 'the past'.

This othering or elsewhereing tendency is apparent in a particular classroom power dynamic: the potential for students (principally, but not always, white students) to atrophy discussion by suggesting that discussion of race and racism is unnecessary, either because:

- race and racism are marginal social problems that happen elsewhere and to other people

- racism is acknowledged to exist but only at very high thresholds

- race is merely an illusion, a categorical error that has been or should be transcended

- to address race and racism is held to exacerbate racism

The four positions broadly categorised above constrain classroom discussion of race. The first three are perhaps most complex, since they open up one black-box (the concept of race) only to reveal another, apparently irreversible black-box inside. The fourth form (exacerbation) might be taken as a simpler shying away. It has been described to me by other Higher Education teachers and by consultants working in Higher Education as having been experienced in two forms. The most direct is a forestalling, either institutional or pedagogic. A race equality consultant related her experience of working with programme deliverers in some Higher Education settings, their attitude is that we don't have problems with race here. It's only when people like you come in from outside that things are stirred up. Another instance was described by the same consultant as originating from some students' reluctance to be placed in the spotlight of the issue. Thus white and black students alike were understandably wary of being involved in discussion that might require them to be held up as exemplars of raced or racist experiences or behaviour, or which might assume that race was the dominant factor in their lived experience. Overcoming this form of reluctance was generally achieved by careful, ethical planning of sessions, which moved beyond black-white binaries to examine multiple expressions of raced experience. The other elsewhereing constraints listed here may well have been rooted, in part, in similar fears. However, the concern in this chapter is not to ascribe psychological motives but to locate these classroom positions discursively.

As suggested previously, race may be represented in classroom discussions as a marginal problem: not necessarily in the sense that it is unimportant but in the sense that it happens elsewhere and to others. This calls to mind attending a symposium on free speech some years ago at a major British academic conference, in which one of the speakers opened his presentation by shouting, 'Nigger!' He went on to make a series of arguments about the distinctions that should be made between language and other forms of action. The use of the racist epithet might be objected to on the grounds that it was ill-mannered, he argued, but that was surely the limit of its harmfulness. After all, no one had been stabbed; no-one had been attacked. Such an argument exemplifies the displacement, the elsewhereing of race. It happens 'over there', in aberrational violence, not 'here' in everyday, vernacular exchanges. This is also an example of the high threshold that is applied to the recognition of raced practices (and racism), another variation of the exoticising tendency. Raced practices will be recognised as raced practices when they pass a certain extreme threshold, such as physical violence.

The marginalisation, the elsewhereing of race is also apparent in what Gillborn (2005: 488) calls the 'avoidance of identifying with a racial experience or group'. The sense in which 'white' raced practices become normalised to the point that they become invisible and are not perceived as constituting a form of race has been examined thoroughly by, for instance, hooks (1992), Bhabha (1994) and Delgado and Stefancic (2000). This is a key form of race as social practice, wherein race is equated with not being white. As a research student, I recall attending a lecture in which the class was informed by the white lecturer that black researchers should not conduct research interviews on issues of race for fear of undermining reliability, since black interviewees would give different answers to black researchers than they would to white researchers on this 'emotive' subject. The comment was not offered as a provocation or as a derogation of the skills of black researchers. Rather, it was an example of white exceptionalism, in which the idea that white researchers were also racialised and were equidistant to this emotive issue was not considered. I would argue that this classroom instance also revealed an epistemology of race because it implied a model in which the practices of white researchers had particular claims on truth and objectivity. In this epistemology, white exceptionalism, elsewhereing and the claim that race is an illusion, a false consciousness overlap.

In one of my own postgraduate taught sessions, during the group discussion that followed the 'what is race?' exercise, a white student, an experienced education professional, exclaimed that he felt uncomfortable with the discussion because, 'I hate thinking of people in terms of race; it's horrible'. This was a variation on the 'I don't think of people as belonging to a race' position, which has also sometimes emerged in similar discussions but it seemed, in this case, to go beyond an opting out and became an opposition to the validity of the discussion. However, while in my taught sessions black students have on occasion claimed a certain colour-blindness (principally with regard to other people), a more common experience has been of some white students professing not only colour-blindness with regard to others but also disclaiming the possibility that they themselves had racial identities.

The historian Scott Malcolmson (2000: 282), in considering early colonial constructions of race, poses the question of why early racial codifications took so long to explicitly name whiteness as a category:

> When we consider that being white brought nothing but power and privileges, we must be struck by the fact that white people were so reluctant to become white. They were, certainly, eager not to be black – to distance themselves from blackness. But they did not mount arguments in favour of whiteness, except by exclusion; that is, whites unlike all others, did not gain their racial characteristics from their race. Their character was a human character.

The silent or transparent nature of whiteness has, in recent times, been subject to extensive criticism by, for example, Hall (1996), who has addressed the senses in which whiteness is able to go unmarked: that is, in which white subjects have the option to ascribe race as the property of non-white others. However, this racial exceptionalism should not be regarded simply as a deception, a discursive trick; it is not only a negative, a denial, but a positive cleaving to a construction of humanism which has deep roots in dimensions of the Enlightenment (Bhabha, 1994; Rizvi and Lingard, 2006). Bhabha's reading of Fanon emphasises that the normalisation of whiteness, its status as universal humanity, is the product of a modernity, whose Enlightenment origins set the terms of what it is to be properly human. This occurred at a historical point when there was little question in European discourses that the human category included whiteness as part of its inalienable content. It is, of course, important to underline that liberal (or, for that matter, radical or conservative) race commonsense is no more uncontested that any other discursive field. However, the Enlightenment's racialised humanism still contains enough purchase to slip into today's everyday understandings of 'progressive' or 'liberal' or 'tolerant' or 'humane' projects.

The pulsation of race

Yet delineating race as something which is neither biologistic fact nor simply an ideological illusion clearly requires the ongoing development of classroom tools for thinking about race. A useful set of tools might be drawn from notions of power and control that have origins in aspects of Bernsteinian thinking. In short, race is a category in itself (a social construct) and its operation depends upon the production and adaptation of myriad sub-categories: such as, black, white, Asian, African, Muslim or Eastern European. This proliferation is even more apparent given the globalisation of racial space, which has generated nuances, anxieties and identities that place race beyond binary categories of black and white (which is not to say that the old binary cannot still be invoked) and incorporate racialised representations of religion, culture and ethnicity.

Classroom work can usefully focus on the shifting boundaries within which raced practices operate. In the modern period, racialised boundaries have shifted over time and global space to produce new race and ethnic categories (Latino/a, African-Caribbean, mixed race, travellers, white Irish). In addition, racialised boundaries become stronger or weaker across epochs (so that in apartheid South Africa racialised boundaries were rendered more or less impermeable) and across particular situations or moments. Thus if we examine, say, Higher Education entry figures in the UK, the boundary between Indian, Chinese and middle class white British populations, boundaries are relatively weak, since all fare well above average. Examination of experiences within Higher Education, however, might reveal stronger boundaries. Importantly, raced boundaries may strengthen momentarily: a White British and a Bangladeshi professional may sit alongside each other in an office performing more or less identical tasks; in applying for promotion, boundaries may thicken.

Asking students to consider how and where raced boundaries are produced may be productive in terms of positioning race as a conceptual problem. It also, of course, requires examination of the content of raced categories. What associations, values, qualities and representations are placed within particular raced categories and what are their consequences for groups and individuals? What content might be present in, say, teachers', students' or researchers' constructions of African-Caribbean boys? What is the content of current news media representations of Muslims or migrant Polish workers? Thus raced boundaries and categories are not static; they pulsate. Race pulsates over historical epochs and everyday moments. Categories such as Latino/a or African-Caribbean exist now where they once did not. At present, in the UK to be a Muslim is a heavily racialised category. There may be times when white Irish and white British categories conflate into a single raced category of whiteness; there are other instances where they decidedly do not (thus the boundary between race and ethnicity also pulsates). These boundaries are further complicated when their intersection with class, gender, sexuality, age and disability is examined.

Conclusion

Understanding raced categories as dynamic, relational and constantly pulsating is a way of pointing to and elaborating upon the changing meaning of race. While race is unintelligible as a biologistic concept, it is something more than an ideological illusion; it carries an objective quality as a cultural artefact or tool that operates through the drawing of boundaries and the inscription of categories. We must also admit that supposedly more fluid or more objective categories, such as ethnicity and culture, are so heavily racialised that they cannot yet, however unappealing we find the fact, supersede the concept of race. The contradiction for educationalists concerned with social justice is that, in using raced categories in research, teaching and institutional development, we are caught in a bind: working both with and against conceptual tools that have yet to be effectively replaced (Gunaratnum, 2003). For the moment, race remains a 'fact' (inverted commas necessary) because of its continued power (inverted commas, sadly, unnecessary). We are not yet post-racial; for that reason, the race concept must be subject to constant interrogation.

Note

1   These estimates are crude, although informed by some recruitment data. For this, I apologise. This chapter is, I stress, a tentative set of reflections that aim to suggest future research possibilities. The figures do, however, provide a rough picture of the teaching groups under discussion. The institution is in the process of refining its data on ethnicity and recruitment.

References

Bhabha, H (1994) *The Location of Culture*. London: Routledge

Cole, M (2004) 'Rule Britannia' and the new American empire. *Policy Futures in Education* 2(3) p523-528

Cole, M (2008) *Marxism and Educational Theory: origins and issues*. London: Routledge

Collins, P (1990) *Black Feminist Thought*. London: Unwin Hyman

Davis, A (1982) *Women, Race and Class*. London: Women's Press

Delgado, R (2003) Crossroads and blind alleys: a critical examination of recent writing about race. *Texas Law Review* 82(1) p121-152.

Delgado, R and Stefancic, J (eds) (2000) *Critical Race Studies: the cutting edge*. Philadelphia: Philadelphia University Press

Fields, B (1990) Slavery, race and ideology in the United States of America. *New Left Review*, 181(May/June) p95-118

Fields, B (2003) Of rogues and geldings, *American Historical Review*, 108 (5) http://history cooperative.press.uiuc.edu/journals/ahr/108.5/fields.html (accessed February 2007)

Fryer, P (1988) *Black People in the British Empire*. London: Pluto

Gillborn, D (2005) Education policy as an act of white supremacy: whiteness, critical race theory and education reform. *Journal of Education Policy* 20(4) p485-505

Gilroy, P (1987) *There Ain't No Black in the Union Jack*. London: Routledge

Gilroy, P (1993) *The Black Atlantic: modernity and double consciousness*. London, Verso

Gilroy, P (2005) Melancholia or conviviality: the politics of belonging in Britain. *Soundings* 29, p35-46.

Goldberg, D (1993) *Racist Culture: philosophy and the politics of meaning*. Oxford: Blackwell

Gunaratnum, Y (2003) *Researching 'Race' and Ethnicity: methods, knowledge and power*. London: Sage

Hall, S (1980) Race, Articulation and Societies Structured in Dominance, UNESCO *Sociological Theories: Race and Colonialism*. Paris: UNESCO

Hall, S (1996) Introduction: who needs identity? In S Hall and P du Gay (eds) *Questions of Cultural Identity*. Sage: London

hooks, b (1990) Postmodern Blackness, *Postmodern Culture*, 1(1) http://www.all4all.org/2004/07/946.shtml (Accessed February 2007)

hooks, b (1992) Representing Whiteness in the Black imagination. In L Grossberg, C Nelson and P Treichler (eds) *Cultural Studies*. London: Routledge

Kundnani, A (2007) *The End of Tolerance?* London: Pluto

Ladson-Billings, G (1998) Just what is critical race theory and what's it doing in a nice field like education? *International Journal of Qualitative Studies in Education* 11(1) p7-24.

Latour, B (1999) Pandora's Hope: essays on the reality of science studies. London: Harvard University Press

Law, J (1992) *Notes on the Theory of Actor Networking: ordering, strategy and heterogeneity*. Lancaster: Centre for Science Studies

Malcolmson, S (2000) *One Drop of Blood: the American misadventure of race*. New York: Farrar, Straus, Giroux

Miles, R (1984) Marxism versus the sociology of 'race relations'. *Ethnic and Racial Studies*, 7(2) p217-237

Miles, R (1989) *Racism*. London: Routledge

Omi, M and Winant, H (1986) *Racial Formation in the United States: from the 1960s to the 1980s*. New York: Routledge

Rizvi, F and Lingard, B (2006) Edward Said and the cultural politics of education. *Discourse: Studies in the Cultural Politics of Education* 27(3) p293-308

Sivanandan, A (1982) *A Different Hunger*. London: Pluto

Winant, H (2000) The theoretical status of the concept of race. In L Back and J Solomos (eds) *Theories of Race and Racism*. London: Routledge

Young, R (2006) Putting materialism back into race theory: towards a transformative theory of race. *The Red Critique* 11, http://www.redcritique.org/WinterSpring2006/putting materialismbackintoracetheory.htm (Accessed February 2007)

Contributors

Norman K. Denzin is Distinguished Professor of Communications, Research Professor of Communications, Cinema Studies, Sociology, Criticism and Interpretive Theory at the University of Illinois, Urbana-Champaign. He is the author, co-author, or co-editor of over 50 books and 200 professional articles and chapters. He is the past President of the Midwest Sociological Society, and the Society for the Study of Symbolic Interaction. He is founding President of the International Association of Qualitative Inquiry and Director of the International Center of Qualitative Inquiry. He is past editor of *The Sociological Quarterly*, founding co-editor of *Qualitative Inquiry* and founding editor of *Cultural Studies-Critical Methodologies* and *Studies in Symbolic Interaction: a Research Annual*.

Frank Furedi is a Professor of Sociology at the University of Kent. His research is oriented towards the study of the impact of precautionary culture and risk aversion on Western societies. In his books he has explored controversies and panics over issues such as health, children, food, new technology and terrorism. At present his research is focused on the way society engages with catastrophes and disasters. His *Invitation to Terror: The Expanding Empire of the Unknown* (2007) deals with these issues.

Susan Heald is Associate Professor and Acting Coordinator of Women's Studies at the University of Manitoba in Winnipeg, Canada. She has been involved in travel/study courses since her undergraduate days more than 30 years ago. The focus of her scholarly work is to explore appropriate pedagogies and politics to facilitate transnational encounters which work against imperial histories and charity discourses to enable genuine solidarity. She has published extensively in the areas of feminist pedagogy and critiques of the university.

159

Ken Montgomery teaches courses in Social Inequality and the Sociology of Education in the Department of Sociology at Wilfrid Laurier University in Waterloo, Ontario, Canada. His research focuses upon the reproduction of normalised structures of domination through collective memories and public representations of national history and culture(s). He has published in *Paedagogica Historica: International Journal of the History of Education, Discourse: Studies in the Cultural Politics of Education* and the *Journal of Peace Education.* He has also taught in the public school systems of Alberta (Canada) and Ibaraki (Japan).

Heather Piper is a Senior Research Fellow at the Education and Social Research Institute at Manchester Metropolitan University, UK. She is a qualitative researcher, and her interests span a broad range of educational and social issues. Her voice in research practice and academic writing is typified by a contrarian approach, a broad based and eclectic intellectual territory in sociology, philosophy, social policy, and a sensitivity to inter-professional concerns informed by her own experiences with the academy.

Fazal Rizvi is a Professor in the Department of Educational Policy Studies at the University of Illinois at Urbana-Champaign, where he directs its Global Studies in Education programme (see: gse.ed.uiuc.edu). Over the past few years, his research has focused on globalisation and education policy and on issues of identity, culture and the internationalisation of education. His new book, co-authored with Bob Lingard, *Globalising Education Policy*, will be published by Routledge in 2008.

James Haywood Rolling, Jr. is a Dual Associate Professor in Art Education and Teaching and Leadership at Syracuse University. Dr. Rolling earned his Ed.D. and Ed.M. in art education at Teachers College, Columbia University. In his earlier education, Dr. Rolling completed his M.F.A. in studio arts research at Syracuse University as a Graduate Fellow in the African American Studies Department, and earned his BFA in visual arts with a minor in creative writing at The Cooper Union School of Art.

David Selby is Professor of Education for Sustainability at the University of Plymouth, England, where he directs the Centre for Sustainable Futures. He was previously (1992-2003) Professor of Education at the

Ontario Institute for Studies in Education of the University of Toronto (OISE/UT) where he was Director of the International Institute for Global Education (IIGE). He has (co)written or (co)edited some twenty books and written over one hundred book chapters and articles. His books include *Global Teacher, Global Learner* (1988), *Earthkind: A Teachers' Handbook on Humane Education* (1995), *In the Global Classroom*, Books One and Two (1999, 2000) and *Weaving Connections: Educating for Peace, Social and Environmental Justice* (2000). His latest book is *Green Frontiers: Environmental Educators Dancing Away from Mechanism* (Rotterdam, Sense, 2008).

Pat Sikes is Professor of Qualitative Inquiry at the School of Education, University of Sheffield. Pat has been involved in research for the best part of 30 years. During that time her focus has been on four inter-related concerns: educators' lives and careers; life history research; qualitative methodologies; and social justice issues. All of these areas are brought together in her chapter for this volume.

Paul Warmington is a Senior Lecturer in Equality, Diversity and Education at the University of Birmingham. He has written and researched extensively around critical understandings of race, widening participation issues, work-related learning and media coverage of education.

Michael Watts is a Senior Research Associate at the Von Hügel Institute, St Edmund's College, Cambridge. His research focuses on widening participation in higher education and the philosophical and sociological dimensions of post-compulsory education.

Index

absolutism 11, 118, 119f
anthropology 71
anti-colonialism *see*
    postcolonialism
anti-positivism *see*
    positivism
antiracism *see* racism
anti-sexism *see* sexism
audit culture 2, 9
autobiography,
    autoethnography 53,
    127f, 129, 133f
autoethnography *see*
    autobiography

capability 99- 110
capital, *see* cultural
    capital
capitalism 22, 121
certainty 114, 118
childhood, children 42,
    56, 58, 86, 134, 139
citizenship education 31,
    122
cognitive dissonance 21,
    24
colonial *see* post
    colonialism
contingency *see*
    essentialism
control *see* surveillance;
    see also power
cross-cultural research 67

cultural imperialism 68
cultures ix, xi, xv, 5, 41,
    54, 67, 119, 120, 124,
    131, 140, 144, 148,
    150
cultural artefact 145, 146
    – bias 10
    – capital 99, 103, 104,
    106, 109
    – coaching xv
    – imagination 43
    – imperialism 68
    – mood 44

democracy 30, 31
denial 18ff, 25, 26, 77
difference *see* other
domination *see* power

empire *see* imperialism
    38, 72, 77, 144, 148,
    156
empiricism 3, 4, 5, 58

epistemology, knowledge,
    knowledge-making 54,
    118, 119
essentialism *see* also facts
    75, 129, 130, 145,
    156
ethical codes, rules,
    planning 70, 71, 79

ethical review xi, 115,
    141
ethics (research) x, 68,
    69, 74, 78

globalisation, globalism
    30f, 120
God, God's eye view xi,
    4, 11, 71, 77

hegemony, hegemonies
    see power
humanism 114, 123f, 154

identity, identity politics,
    personhood 38, 45,
    53, 72, 87f, 113, 118,
    127-141
imperialism (*see also*
    cultural imperialism)
    xiv, 69, 73, 113, 124,
    149
indigenous knowledge *see*
    epistemology

intellectual 63, 113, 117,
    120f, 123, 125
interculturalism *see*
    cultures
Islam 115, 116f, 119,
    150, 156

knowledge, knowledge-
making *see*
epistemology

life history 99, 104, 110
linguistic capital *see*
cultural capital
localism 29f, 31

moral panic 51, 54f
multiculturalism xiv, 83,
87f, 93ff,
Muslim *see* Islam

names, naming 131-133,
138, 140f
narrative, narrative
capital *see also* voice
99ff, 102, 105ff, 130,
134
nation, nationalism,
nationality,
nationhood,
patriotism 85ff, 94,
114, 117f, 134, 148

objective inquiry,
objectivity 6, 22, 55,
124, 127, 128, 156
ordering *see* surveillance
Other, Othering, 'us and
them' 28, 119, 126,
127, 150

patriotism *see* nation
policing *see* surveillance
politics of evidence *see*
evidence
positivism 71, 73, 75
post-colonialism 70, 71,
76, 79, 116, 119
power, hegemony ix, xii,
19, 35, 72, 78, 85,
99f, 116, 118, 121,
131, 140, 144, 155

pseudo-science *see* science
public intellectuals *see*
intellectual

qualitative research x, xiv,
1, 2, 4, 6f, 76, 128
quantitative research ixf,
xi

race, racism, anti-racism
xvi, 69, 70, 72, 73,
79, 83ff, 134ff, 143-
155
rationality 27
regulation 59, 60
relativism *see* absolutism
research ethics, *see* ethics,
research
research methods,
methodologies 1-12,
73, 77
rhetoric 36, 44, 46, 47f,
53

science, scientific method,
pseudo-science 71, 77,
78, 145, 150
self, self-image *see*
identity
sexism, anti-sexism 70,
73
silence *see* voice
social capital *see* cultural
capital
social justice 63, 117, 156
speaking *see* voice
standards 3, 5f
story *see* narrative
subjectivity *see* objectivity
surveillance, control,
ordering, policing 56,
57, 62

truth 114, 123, 130

us and them *see* othering

voice xv, 53, 108, 110,
115f, 117, 121, 133
vulnerability xii, xiiif, 35-
48, 56, 59, 77